AMERICANS
THE *Spirit* OF A *Nation*

BILLY the KID

"It Was a Game of Two and I Got There First"

Paul B. Thompson

Enslow Publishers, Inc.
40 Industrial Road
Box 398
Berkeley Heights, NJ 07922
USA

http://www.enslow.com

For Glennie and Toni

Copyright © 2010 by Paul B. Thompson

Library of Congress Cataloging-in-Publication Data

Thompson, Paul B.
   Billy the Kid : "It was a game of two and I got there first" / Paul B. Thompson.
    p. cm. — (Americans. The spirit of a nation)
     Summary: "Examines the short, violent life of Billy the Kid, including his
childhood, the beginning of his criminal life, his showdowns with the law, and his
rise to a myth and legend in the Old American West"—Provided by publisher.
   Includes bibliographical references and index.
   ISBN-13: 978-0-7660-3480-8
   ISBN-10: 0-7660-3480-1
    1. Billy, the Kid—Juvenile literature. 2. Outlaws—Southwest, New—Biography—
Juvenile literature. 3. Southwest, New—Biography—Juvenile literature. I. Title.
   F786.B54T494 2010
   364.15'52092—dc22
   [B]
                              2009012124

Printed in the United States of America

102009 Lake Book Manufacturing, Inc., Melrose Park, IL

10 9 8 7 6 5 4 3 2 1

To Our Readers:
We have done our best to make sure all Internet Addresses in this book were active
and appropriate when we went to press. However, the author and the publisher have
no control over and assume no liability for the material available on those Internet
sites or on other Web sites they may link to. Any comments or suggestions can be sent
by e-mail to comments@enslow.com or to the address on the back cover.

♻ Enslow Publishers, Inc., is committed to printing our books on recycled paper. The
paper in every book contains 10% to 30% post-consumer waste (PCW). The cover
board on the outside of each book contains 100% PCW. Our goal is to do our part to
help young people and the environment too!

Illustration Credits: © Andrew Woodley / Alamy, p. 114; Arizona Historical Society,
pp. 78, 83, 93; Associated Press, pp. 8, 42, 95, 113; © Collection of the New-York
Historical Society, USA / The Bridgeman Art Library, p. 63; Enslow Publishers, Inc.,
p. 18; Everett Collection, p. 16; The Granger Collection, New York, pp. 10, 14, 22, 34,
56, 73, 80; Library of Congress, pp. 1, 4, 20, 25, 29, 44, 49, 58, 60, 71, 106, 110;
Courtesy Museum of New Mexico, pp. 98, 104; National Archives and Records
Administration, pp. 67, 69; © North Wind Picture Archives, pp. 12, 90; Printroom.com,
pp. 27, 51; © Shutterstock®, pp. 86, 97; Special Collections, University of Arizona
Library, Papers of Walter Noble Burns, pp. 30, 37, 46.

Cover Illustration: Everett Collection (Portrait of Billy the Kid).

CONTENTS

Billy the Kid

Chapter 1

The Smell of Bacon

Early in the morning of December 23, 1880, five men huddled in a cold, dark stone sheep-herder's hut in Stinking Springs, New Mexico Territory. All were wanted men, hunted by the law. Snow was falling, and they had eaten and slept little. The outlaws had fled the scene of an ambush just four days before. They had ridden into Fort Sumner, hoping to surprise and rout a posse of lawmen who were on their trail, but they were the ones surprised. The posse was stronger than they had heard, led by Pat Garrett, the sheriff of Lincoln County. In a fast exchange of shots, one outlaw, Tom O'Folliard, was killed and another bandit lost his horse. The rest rode for their lives. Their leader, but not their boss, was a twenty-one-year-old gun-man who went by the name William H. Bonney. Everyone knew him as Billy the Kid.

What Was Billy the Kid's Real Name?

During his life, Billy the Kid used a variety of names. At the time of his death he was generally known as William H. Bonney. At other times he was known as Billy Bonney, Kid Antrim, or other variations of these names. His birth name was Henry McCarty. When his mother married William Antrim in 1873, Billy began using his stepfather's name. Billy's brother Joe is sometimes referred to as Joe Antrim and sometimes Joe McCarty. "Kid" was a nickname Billy acquired because of his youth and boyish appearance.

By 1877, when the Kid was deeply involved in a criminal gang, he adopted the alias "William H. Bonney."[1] No one knows where he got the name—he may have just made it up. But many people thought Bonney was his real name and Antrim an alias.

The outlaws stopped briefly at a ranch for food, then set out for the nearby hill country. Sheriff Garrett waited a day or so to pursue them, keeping warm and dry in town while Billy and his comrades shivered in the snow. On December 21, the posse left Fort Sumner. They tracked the outlaws to the old stone hut three miles from the Wilcox ranch. At three o'clock in the morning of December 23, Garrett's posse surrounded the tiny shelter.

Asleep inside the hut were Billy the Kid, Dave Rudabaugh, Charlie Bowdre, Tom Pickett, and Billy Wilson. Creeping up in the darkness the lawmen could hear the outlaws snoring. The posse waited until dawn. At that point one man emerged from the lone door, wearing a wide-brimmed sombrero. Since the Kid was known to favor that sort of hat, everyone in the posse thought it was Billy. The posse opened fire, killing not Billy the Kid but Charlie Bowdre.

Finding they were trapped, the outlaws tried to draw in their horses tethered nearby. They hoped to get them close enough to the hut to jump on them and ride away. Garrett shot one horse, who fell directly in front of the hut's only door.[2] With well-aimed shots he cut the ropes holding the others, and the horses trotted away from danger.

Billy and Garrett traded rough banter for a while. Garrett called out to Billy: how was he doing?

"Pretty well, but we have no wood to get breakfast with," Billy replied.

Garrett said, "Come out and get some. Be a little sociable."

Pat Garrett is shown in this undated photo. Garrett had Billy the Kid trapped inside the sheepherder's hut.

"Can't do it, Pat. Business is too confining. No time to run around."[3]

Garrett next teased Billy about his failed attempt to drive the lawmen out of Fort Sumner. Billy would not be baited, and he and his friends sat tight behind the stone walls.

The outlaws tried to burrow through one of the stone walls to get out, but the posse peppered the site with rifle fire until the digging stopped.

The lawmen did not want to storm the place. Forcing the single entrance would spill a lot of blood. Garrett decided on a siege. It was bitterly cold, and the outlaws had no heat and apparently no food. Feeding his men in shifts, Garrett let the smell of coffee and frying bacon waft over the hut. That did it. At about 4 P.M., a white flag appeared. The outlaws surrendered on Garrett's promise that they would be protected from reprisals. Garrett gave his word. One of the posse wanted to shoot Billy on sight, and only on the threat of his own death did he back down.[4]

On Christmas Eve, 1880, Pat Garrett loaded his prisoners in a wagon shackled together and started down the cold road to Las Vegas, New Mexico Territory, to face trial and final judgment.

City Boy

Billy the Kid's exact date and place of birth are unknown. It is generally thought that he was born in New York City in 1859. His mother was an Irish immigrant. Starting in the 1840s, millions of Irish people left their homeland when a great potato famine gripped the country. It appears that Billy's mother, Catherine McCarty, was born in 1829. She may have arrived in New York in 1846, but it is very hard to prove exactly when she arrived because her name was a common one. Many Catherine McCartys turned up in the United States, driven out of Ireland by poverty and hunger.

Born in the City

According to New York City records, a couple named Patrick and Catherine McCarty had a son, Henry, born September 17, 1859. Another Catherine McCarty with a son named Henry (born November 20, 1859) had no husband listed in the same records.[1] Henry McCarty's father may have been missing, dead, or simply not married to his mother. In any case, the future Billy the Kid was born Henry McCarty, and lived the first years of his life in the slums of New York. Billy had a brother, Joseph, who had been born either in 1854 or 1863—exact facts remain unknown. Nothing else is known about his family, who lived in New York during the Civil War (1861–1865).

By 1865, Catherine McCarty and her two sons had moved to Indianapolis, Indiana. Little information on the boys' father remains. Catherine told local officials in Indiana she was a widow, and gave her late husband's name as Michael McCarty.[2]

While in Indianapolis, Catherine met William Henry Antrim, a Union army veteran. After the war, Antrim delivered packages for an express company. How he and Catherine McCarty met is not known, but he followed her and the boys when they moved to Marion County, Indiana, in 1866. By 1870, the McCartys and "Uncle Bill" Antrim were in Wichita, Kansas. Catherine

Immigrants landing in New York City in the 1850s. Billy's mother, Catherine McCarty, was an Irish immigrant who may have arrived in New York City in 1846.

McCarty operated a very successful clothes-cleaning business, the City Laundry. She and Bill seemed to be getting ahead, making a living and buying property, when disaster struck. Catherine McCarty fell ill with tuberculosis.

Tuberculosis, called TB or consumption, is a terrible disease. It affects the lungs, gradually destroying them. Progress of the disease can take years, and in those days there was no cure. The best way to lengthen a TB patient's life was to move to a higher, drier climate. In June 1871, Catherine sold her property in Wichita and moved to Denver, Colorado, with her boys and Uncle Bill. They did not remain in Denver long, moving on to Silver City in the sparsely settled New Mexico Territory.[3] New Mexico was part of a large tract of land the United States had won in the Mexican War of 1846–1848. When the McCartys moved there it was not yet a state, but a federally administered territory.

Moving to New Mexico

At first New Mexico was good for the McCartys. Catherine ran a boarding house in Silver City, where she was remembered by a neighbor as a "jolly Irish lady, full of life and mischief."[4] Bill Antrim prospected for silver, without any great success. But things went well enough for him to formally marry Catherine on March 1, 1873. Henry and Joseph were witnesses to the wedding, held in the First Presbyterian Church of Santa Fe. At the time they married, Bill Antrim was thirty and Catherine was forty-three. Henry McCarty, the future Billy the Kid, was thirteen years old.

It was probably while living in Silver City that young Billy began his lifelong affection for Latino people and culture. New Mexico was predominately Latino, and while many Anglo-Americans were contemptuous of their Latino neighbors, Billy was not. He learned to speak Spanish fluently. He enjoyed local music and dancing (he was said to be a skillful dancer), and admired Latina girls. Along with his boyish enthusiasms, Billy's early years in New Mexico were quite normal. Later in life, many of his schoolmates and neighbors spoke of him as a good kid, inclined to mischief, but hardly a born desperado. Most of his peers agreed that Henry Antrim, the future outlaw Billy the Kid, was a pretty nice boy.

A wagon train traveling to New Mexico. The McCartys moved to the New Mexico Territory in the early 1870s. For quite some time, Billy lived a normal childhood in Silver City.

The Antrim family's happiness did not last long. Catherine's health suddenly worsened as tuberculosis destroyed her lungs. She died on September 16, 1874.[5] Henry was fourteen, and now had only his stepfather Bill Antrim as his guardian.

Billy the Kid was small for his age. A boyhood friend described him as "very slender . . . undersized and really girlish looking. I don't think he weighed over seventy-five pounds."[6]

After his mother died, Henry lived with the parents of his schoolmate Chauncey Truesdell. Chauncey's father ran the Star Hotel in Silver City, New Mexico. Henry earned his keep by waiting on tables in the hotel's dining room and washing dishes. Bill Antrim also found him work in a butcher shop. Henry continued to attend school, and boarded with

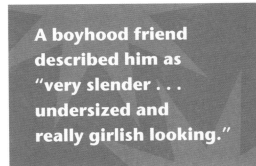

A boyhood friend described him as "very slender . . . undersized and really girlish looking."

others' parents around town. Bill Antrim got along well enough with his stepson, but he did not exert much control over the boy. He was busy trying to strike it rich prospecting for silver.

On the Run

It did not take long for Henry to stray. A local character called Sombrero Jack (real name: George Shaffer) stole a bundle of clothing from a local Chinese laundry. He gave the clothing to Henry and another boy to hide. Sombrero Jack claimed it was just a prank, but the sheriff

Was Billy Left-handed?

In a famous tintype photograph taken in 1880, Billy poses with a Winchester rifle and Colt revolver. Because tintypes show a reversed image, many people seeing the picture later assumed Billy was left-handed. He appears to wear his revolver on his left hip. Today, it is known that the image was reversed. The loading gate on the Winchester Model 1873 rifle was always on the right side, never the left as in most prints of Billy's picture. Reversing the image restores the loading gate to the correct position and shows Billy was right-handed after all.

Left-handedness was once regarded as a sign of an evil nature. The word "sinister," which in modern English means "threatening harm, evil, or misfortune" is actually a Latin word meaning left-handed. The idea comes from Roman fortune-tellers, who interpreted omens on their left as being tokens of bad luck.

The legend that Billy was left-handed influenced the title of a popular film about him made in 1958 called *The Left Handed Gun*, starring Paul Newman.[7]

Paul Newman holding a gun in his left hand in The Left Handed Gun, *as legend said that Billy was left-handed.*

arrested Henry Antrim for his part in the deed. He decided to put the boy in jail to scare him.

It did not work. Henry escaped. He wormed his way up an unused chimney. Convinced he was now a genuine fugitive, he fled to Arizona to escape punishment.[8] No one in Silver City thought he was a criminal, just a boy who got involved with the wrong sort of man and took the blame for another's deed. Without his mother to guide him, Henry followed his instincts. His instincts told him to run.

He was just fifteen, small but wiry, clever and charming. Finding work in Arizona as a ranch hand for W. J. "Sorghum" Smith, Henry also drove a team of horses for Army captain G. C. Smith at Camp Grant. He delivered supplies and lumber to the post. As many men did in the West, he learned to use a revolver. The territory was wide open, with many lawless types on the loose. Driving a wagon full of valuable supplies, Henry needed to know how to use a gun for self-defense.

The Kid's First Gunfight

In Arizona, Henry met a blacksmith named Frank P. Cahill. He was known as "Windy" Cahill because he was a loud, blustering man. He was a bully, too, and soon began picking on the youngster from New Mexico. Henry took Cahill's insults for a while, until one night in Adkins' dance hall when they were playing cards. Cahill badgered Henry, calling him ugly names. The boy replied in kind. Outraged, the blacksmith attacked Henry and wrestled him to the ground. Struggling in

At just fifteen, Billy the Kid was on the run in the New Mexico Territory.
For the remainder of his life, he spent all of his time in different places
in the area. This is a map of the important places in Billy's life.

the older man's grip, Henry pulled his .45 revolver and shot Cahill in the stomach.[9] Windy Cahill died the following day.

The justice of the peace for Bonito, Arizona, was Miles Wood. He was also Henry's landlord. Wood arrested Henry Antrim, "alias Kid," and confined him to the army guardhouse at Camp Grant. Wood held an inquiry into Cahill's death and ruled that the shooting was a criminal act and not self-defense.

As in Silver City, the Kid did not stay locked up for long. He escaped, possibly with a sympathetic soldier's help.[10] He then stole a fast horse and rode quickly back to New Mexico. The career of the notorious outlaw had begun.

> Struggling in the older man's grip, Henry pulled his .45 revolver and shot Cahill in the stomach.

3

Lincoln County

On the run from the law after the killing of Windy Cahill, Henry or Kid Antrim headed for New Mexico. Because he was raised by a mother and stepfather from back East, where people were more settled and laws more enforced, he may have thought he was in worse trouble than he really was. His part in the Chinese laundry robbery was not a serious crime. There is no evidence he was wanted in New Mexico for petty theft, or even for his escape from jail. Shooting Cahill was a much more serious matter. But the blacksmith's reputation as a bully and his frequent abuse of the Kid convinced many the killing was self-defense. Law enforcement in the western territories was frequently spotty. Common ideas of justice and honor often trumped written law. Henry apparently did not realize how casual local attitudes were about crime. Seeing himself as an outlaw, though, he decided to live as an outlaw.

Mastering His Outlaw Skills

Still only fifteen years old, he had been riding horses, driving teams, and learning to use a gun for over a year. These were normal skills to master on the frontier, but Henry worked on them with more than passing interest. Being small, there was always the chance he would be picked on by bigger, meaner types like Cahill. Being good on a horse protected him from the jeers of his hard-riding comrades. Handling a gun well was even more important. A man was expected to stand up to insults, real or imagined, and the gun usually ended all arguments. For fun the Kid gambled and pursued girls, but he avoided two common adult vices. Henry did not smoke tobacco, and he drank alcohol sparingly.[1]

As Kid Antrim matured he never lost his slight, boyish looks. Fully grown he was five-feet, seven-inches tall, weighed about 135 pounds, and had curly brown hair and bright blue eyes. In an age of big beards and extravagant mustaches he was usually clean shaven. His most notable feature, aside from his eyes, were his

As a young teenager, Billy the Kid became a true American frontiersman like the one pictured here. He mastered riding horses, driving cattle, and using a gun.

prominent front teeth. These gave him a rather disarming smile. Kid Antrim smiled a lot.

His appearance was deceptive. Even at the height of his fame as Billy the Kid, some people were prone to not taking him seriously. The small, smiling young man did not seem dangerous.

Joining "the Boys"

The Kid settled in 1875 in a region called Lincoln County. Organized by the territorial legislature in 1869,

Lincoln County was a vast area, thinly populated, dotted with small towns and large cattle herds. Nine years after its founding, Lincoln County had grown in size until it made up one-fourth of the New Mexico Territory.[2]

On the run from Arizona, Kid Antrim stopped at Apache Tejo, a small town south of Silver City. The site of an abandoned army fort, Apache Tejo had become a haven for outlaws.[3] Before long, Kid Antrim had joined a criminal gang known as "the Boys." The boss of the Boys was Jesse Evans, a former cowboy who had worked for cattle baron John Chisum.[4]

In 1877, Evans was about twenty-five years old. His band of desperadoes roamed the territory, robbing, rustling (stealing) cattle, and causing general mayhem. In one notorious episode, Evans and an ally, a crooked cattleman named John Kinney, were beaten up and thrown out of a dance hall in Las Cruces by some angry U.S. Army soldiers. Bested by fists, Evans and Kinney returned with guns and killed three men, one of whom was an innocent bystander. They were never prosecuted for the deaths.[5]

The Name Change

This was the violent man Henry Antrim joined. Along the way from Arizona he had acquired a new name, William H. Bonney. Despite research by historians to find the origins of this name, it appears Henry Antrim simply made it up to disguise his identity. He had a criminal record in New Mexico already, even if it was only for petty theft and jailbreaking. His Kid nickname lingered on, and in three years it would blend with the Bonney alias to become Billy the Kid.

Billy became one of the Boys. Men came and went from the gang, though at times as many as two dozen men might ride together. They halted stagecoaches, looking for gold. The gang descended on taverns, ate and drank all they wanted, then dared the owner to try to collect payment from them. There was no organized force for law and order in this part of New Mexico strong enough to resist them, and the Boys knew it.

After one wild ride around Lincoln County, Evans made a speech to his men. They elected him "colonel" of their gang, as was the custom in militia companies. They also passed a number of noisy, pointless resolutions about their likes and dislikes. Their last proclamation carried a warning: "[T]he public is our oyster, and that having the power, we claim the right to appropriate any property we may take a fancy to."[6]

> "[T]he public is our oyster, and that having the power, we claim the right to appropriate any property we may take a fancy to."

Evans had an important ally in Lincoln County, John H. Riley, a partner in James J. Dolan & Co. This firm operated a large general store in the town of Lincoln, and had a monopoly on trade for miles around. Without competition, the Dolan store, called "the House," charged high prices, and when people could not afford to pay, they extended credit to their

The Boys often halted stagecoaches, looking for gold.
This photo shows two stagecoaches from the 1880s.

customers. Many people in Lincoln ran up large debts to the House.[7]

Besides the store, Dolan & Co. had contracts to sell cattle and supplies to the U.S. Army. Through government agents they also supplied beef to the Apache Indian reservation. Jesse Evans and the Boys sometimes stole cattle, then sold them to Dolan & Co., which in turn sold them to the Indian agency or the Army.

Start of the Lincoln County War

Not even an outfit as powerful as the Boys could operate freely forever. On October 17, 1877, a posse of angry Lincoln County men surrounded the Boys' hideout and took Evans prisoner, along with three of his men. They were put in jail in Lincoln to await trial.

About thirty members of the Boys, including Billy, gathered in Lincoln in early November to plot Evans' escape. When he entered Lincoln for the first time, Billy became part of the events that led to the infamous Lincoln County War.

Basically, there were two sides in this complicated story: Jimmy Dolan of Dolan & Co., with John H. Riley and the authorities in Lincoln, versus rancher and businessman John Tunstall, his lawyer Alexander McSween, and those people in the county who opposed the monopoly of the House. At stake was the wealth and business of much of New Mexico.

> **Tunstall wrote to his parents in England that he wanted "half of every dollar made in the county by *anyone*."**

John Tunstall, twenty-four years old, was a wealthy, educated Englishman who had come to the American West to enlarge his fortune. He was not romantic or idealistic about searching for riches in the United States. Tunstall was frankly out for money and power, and he was prepared to be as ruthless as Jimmy Dolan or Jesse Evans to get it. Tunstall wrote to his parents in England that he wanted "half of every dollar made in the county by *anyone*."[8]

The commercial rivalry between Dolan and Tunstall was straightforward. More complicated are the shifting alliances and friendships between the supporters of the two sides. Evans was Riley's partner in crime, so it was

Jimmy Dolan (above) was a powerful man in Lincoln County. Billy the Kid joined Dolan's business rival, John Tunstall.

natural Riley would want to see Evans freed. As "colonel" of the Boys, Evans had a lot of power in Lincoln County, so while he was in jail, John Tunstall paid him a friendly visit. Tunstall brought gifts of whiskey and clothes, and did his best to make friends with the outlaw chief.[9]

Billy Changes His Course

Billy Bonney, with a large number of the Boys, helped Jesse Evans break out of jail on November 17, 1877.

The lone guard on duty was easily overcome, and the group freed Evans. The Boys rode to a ranch operated by Dick Brewer, who worked for John Tunstall. They repaid Tunstall's hospitality by stealing some of Tunstall's horses before departing for the Pecos River region. Having helped free his boss, Billy did not follow Evans to the Pecos. He had his mind on a different course.

Whatever bad decisions Billy had made in his life, he was not blind to his own advancement. Under Evans, he was just one of the Boys. Billy got to know Dick Brewer, and saw he might better his lot by throwing in with Tunstall. Billy would not be one of a lawless gang, but a hired hand. He would also be a soldier in a cause. Tunstall aimed to break the hold of Dolan & Co. over Lincoln County, and for that task he needed gunfighters.

The Regulators

Working for John Tunstall was a new experience for Billy. Though he had had honest jobs before, they had been menial ones like washing dishes or waiting tables. His on-again, off-again work as a cowboy had been marred by accusations of cattle rustling. But as 1877 drew to a close, Billy Bonney had the most comfortable time in his life. He had a place in the bunkhouse, three meals a day, and wages in his pocket. On the Tunstall ranch, he had friends who were not roving outlaws, like the

John Tunstall hired Billy the Kid as a ranch hand. However, the Kid's main purpose was working as a private soldier.

Coe cousins George and Frank, and Charlie Bowdre and his Latina wife, Manuela. Another good friend was Josiah "Doc" Scurlock, who had studied medicine in New Orleans before giving it up for a footloose life out West.[1]

George and Frank Coe played fiddle and Billy Bonney "sang like a bird."

Billy was well known for his love of singing and dancing. He spoke excellent Spanish, and mixed well with his Latino neighbors. George Coe remarked late in life that several nights a week Billy and his many friends would have a "singing," where George and Frank Coe played fiddle and Billy Bonney "sang like a bird."[2]

A Private Soldier

No one had any illusions about Billy's role. Though hired as a ranch hand to herd cattle, his real purpose was to fill out the ranks of Tunstall's private army. For years Billy had practiced with the best firearms available: the .44-caliber Colt revolver, known as the Peacemaker, and the Model 1873 Winchester lever-action rifle. He was quick and accurate on horseback or on foot. At one point he switched from the Peacemaker to a newer model, the .41-caliber Colt "Thunderer." The .41 Colt was a double-action gun, meaning it could be fired simply by pulling the trigger. The Peacemaker had to be cocked with the thumb before it could be fired. In theory, the Thunderer was faster-shooting, though its mechanism was more delicate than the rugged Peacemaker's.

Frontier Firearms

Firearms have a long association with the American frontier. Guns were a necessary tool of survival in a lawless territory. For some in the Wild West, guns were tools of profit and power.

The basic handgun of the era was a six-shot revolver, usually .44 or .45 caliber. During the Civil War (1861–1865), revolvers were loaded with loose blackpowder, round lead balls, and single percussion caps to detonate each shot. By the end of the war, self-contained cartridges, such as are still used today, were common.

Large revolvers like the Colt Model 1873 or the Smith and Wesson "Schofield" were single-action types. This means the hammer had to be drawn back and locked before the trigger could be pulled to fire the gun. Double-action guns, like Billy's Colt Thunderer, could be fired simply by squeezing the trigger.

Rifles ranged from large, single-shot weapons, designed to bring down buffalo at long distance, to light repeating carbines that used the same ammunition as common revolvers. The Model 1873 Winchester was the most famous rifle of this kind. By operating a lever behind the trigger it was possible to fire a dozen shots or more without reloading.

Shotguns were much favored by outlaws and lawmen alike. Two barrels of heavy lead pellets could do great damage at close range. Ten- and twelve-gauge shotguns had their barrels shortened to make them easier to carry. Short barrels also encouraged the shot to spread more when fired.[3]

Other gunmen hired on with Tunstall. Among them was Henry Brown, a former buffalo hunter, and Fred Waite, who was part Choctaw Indian. Waite and Billy the Kid became good friends. They often spoke of operating their own ranch together one day. It was a dream they never would achieve. Events in Lincoln County quickly reached a crisis point.

At first, Tunstall's struggle with the House was financial and legal. Tunstall opened a rival store to compete with Dolan & Co. By January 1878, his cash flow dried up and he had to mortgage the store, its inventory, and even the land it stood on. He needed the money to fight a court case brought against him and his lawyer, Alexander McSween, in Mesilla, New Mexico. The judge ordered their property seized as security against the suit for ten thousand dollars. William Brady, sheriff of Lincoln County and a friend of Jimmy Dolan's, confiscated McSween's property and took over Tunstall's store. The Englishman's only remaining assets were the horses and cattle at his ranch. It was only a matter of time before Dolan and the sheriff tried to take hold of Tunstall's livestock.

Billy and his comrades were constantly on guard, facing off against Sheriff Brady's deputies and gunmen who were paid by the House to grab Tunstall's stock. Dolan hired even more guns. His band grew to fifty armed men, many of whom were former members of Jesse Evans' gang, the Boys. He could also rely on Sheriff Brady and his deputies to enforce his will in Lincoln.

Some of the men Billy the Kid worked with in Tunstall's group, including Henry Brown, were former buffalo hunters. The Kid would encounter many former buffalo hunters in his life. This is an engraving of a buffalo hunter in the 1870s.

A Brutal Murder

On February 18, 1878, Tunstall decided to take a small herd of horses to Lincoln to sell. He was escorted by his best and toughest men: Billy the Kid, Henry Brown, John Middleton, Robert Widenmann, and Dick Brewer. After they left the ranch, a posse arrived from Lincoln. Jimmy Dolan, deputized by Sheriff Brady, led the posse to Tunstall's place to seize any valuable livestock to hold against the $10,000 civil judgment. Finding Tunstall gone, part of the posse went after him.

By afternoon, Tunstall's bodyguards, lulled by an uneventful ride, spotted a flock of wild turkeys. The Englishman's hired guns scattered in pursuit of the flock, leaving their young boss to guard the horse herd alone. Suddenly, the posse from Lincoln came riding up. Those of his men still in sight shouted for Tunstall to flee, but the young Englishman would not. He rode up to the Dolan posse, ready to talk.

Tunstall was barely close enough to be heard when one of Dolan's men, Buck Morton, raised his rifle and shot Tunstall off his horse. Another Dolan gunman, Tom Hill, got off his horse and killed the Englishman with a shot from Tunstall's own pistol at close range. To add insult to his murderous deed, Hill also shot Tunstall's fine bay horse.

Scattered around the plain, Billy and the others could not help their boss. Hearing shots and spying Tunstall's fall, they gathered together to face an expected attack by the Dolan posse. Sizing up their alerted enemies, the House gang rode away.

The brutal murder of Tunstall started the Lincoln County War in earnest. When Tunstall's body was brought to Alexander McSween's house for viewing before burial, Billy the Kid was heard to say to his dead employer, "I'll get some of them before I die."[4]

Forming the Regulators

Tunstall employed forty gunmen at the time of his death. His partner, McSween, a lawyer and not a fighter, tried to bring Tunstall's killers to justice legally. He also wanted to get control of Tunstall's assets back from Sheriff Brady. Most local law officers and judges were controlled by the House, but McSween found a justice of the peace, John B. Wilson, who was ready to issue warrants for the arrest of Tunstall's murderers. Wilson deputized Billy the Kid, Fred Waite, and a constable named Martinez, who went to Dolan's store to serve the warrants. It was a bold move, but foolhardy. Waiting in the House was Sheriff Brady and his deputies, guns drawn. Instead of arresting the sheriff for his part in seizing Tunstall's property, Billy and his companions found themselves disarmed and marched to jail.

Frightened by the power of his enemies, McSween fled Lincoln for a hideout in the mountains. Dick Brewer, foreman of Tunstall's ranch, was made of sterner stuff. Under the authority of Justice Wilson, Brewer was

> Billy the Kid was heard to say to his dead employer, "I'll get some of them before I die."

Sheriff William Brady fought against Tunstall and Billy the Kid in the Lincoln County War.

named a special constable for Lincoln. He quickly organized Tunstall's hired guns into a posse of his own. He called them the Regulators. ("Regulator" was a term going back to the days before the American Revolution. It meant someone who tried to restore law and order. In fact, Regulator was a fancy name for a vigilante.)

"The Iron Clad"

Anywhere from ten to fifty men rode with the Regulators. The core of the group included Billy Bonney,

Henry Brown, Charlie Bowdre, Fred Waite, Doc Scurlock, the Coes, and John Middleton. The most serious members of the group took an oath among themselves never to reveal any information about the doings of the Regulators. This hard core of twelve gunmen called their oath "the Iron Clad."[5]

The Iron Clads had no faith in McSween's legal maneuvers. They wanted revenge. Number one on their list was the man who first shot John Tunstall, Buck Morton. A band of Regulators caught Morton on March 6, 1878, and chased him on horseback for five miles. A hundred shots were fired at the fleeing Morton. When his horse finally gave out, Morton surrendered on condition that the Regulators not kill him. The Regulators started back for Lincoln with their captive. Fearful of assassination, Morton grabbed a pistol from one of his captors, shot him, and tried to escape. He and another Dolan posse member, Frank Baker, were gunned down. Billy the Kid was present, and undoubtedly fired at the men. But Morton and Baker were hit many times, so their deaths cannot be counted exclusively to Billy's "score."

In the meantime, McSween's attempts to make the Regulators a legal group failed. The governor of New Mexico territory, Samuel Axtell, denied Justice Wilson's authority to appoint lawmen. Sheriff Brady was the top lawman in Lincoln County once more—but not for long. The Iron Clads decided they had seen enough of Dolan's ally. On March 31, six of them lay in wait behind an adobe (mud brick) wall in Lincoln. Waite, Brown, Frank McNab, Middleton, Jim French, and Billy Bonney crouched there until the next morning. When Sheriff Brady and four of his deputies came strolling down the street, the Regulators stood up and opened fire.

Brady was cut down along with one deputy. The other lawmen ran, catching bullets as they fled. One of them, Billy Matthews, fired back, hitting Billy the Kid and Jim French in the legs. The two groups finally drew apart, and firing stopped. The Regulators did not flee, but remained in town while Billy and Jim French sought medical attention for their wounds. When they did ride out, Brady's deputies fired at them—from long range, so no one else was hit. Not knowing if the Regulators meant to come back, Brady's surviving deputies called for help from the U.S. Army. By that afternoon a troop of cavalry was in Lincoln to enforce the peace.[6]

More Revenge

The Regulators had struck back for their dead leader, but they were not done yet. Next on their list for justice was Andrew L. Roberts, known as "Buckshot" Roberts because a shotgun was his favorite weapon. In a land of colorful characters, Roberts was an unusual fellow. Like Henry Brown, he had once been a buffalo hunter. It was said he once had a shootout with some Texas Rangers and still carried a load of buckshot in his shoulder from the encounter. He was squat and powerfully built, and liked to ride mules instead of horses. Roberts was part of the posse that went to John Tunstall's ranch the day he was murdered, but he was not in the group that killed the Englishman. Why Roberts was singled out is not clear—it is possible one of the Regulators may have had a personal grudge against him.

When Roberts received word that the Regulators wanted him, he wisely decided to leave Lincoln County. He sold his small ranch on the upper Ruidoso River. Roberts expected final payment by mail, and on April 4 he rode to Blazer's Mill to get his money.

> **"The Kid is with you and he will kill me on sight."**

Blazer's Mill was a large adobe house owned by dentist J. H. Blazer. Mail for outlying areas was delivered there. When Roberts came riding in on his mule, Dr. Blazer warned him to keep moving. Armed men had been seen west of the station. Blazer and Roberts both suspected the Regulators were on his trail—and they were right.

Standoff With "Buckshot" Roberts

Dick Brewer had fourteen men with him, the Iron Clads. Billy the Kid was riding even though he had a painful wound in one thigh from the ambush that killed Sheriff Brady. Roberts cleared out of Blazer's Mill ahead of them, but when he spotted the mail carrier headed for the dentist's house, he went back to get his money. The Iron Clads saw him. Frank Coe knew Roberts well, and went out to talk to him. Leaving his pistol on his mule as a courtesy to Dr. Blazer, Roberts went to meet Coe carrying his Winchester rifle. Coe asked Roberts to surrender without a fight, but Buckshot would not listen to him.

He said to Coe, "The Kid is with you and he will kill me on sight."[7]

Coe promised to protect Roberts, but he would not give himself up. After half an hour, Dick Brewer grew impatient and sent some Regulators outside to take Roberts by force.

Charlie Bowdre ordered Roberts to surrender. Buckshot replied simply "No," raised his Winchester to his hip and fired. Bowdre fired at the exact same moment. His bullet hit Roberts in the stomach. Buckshot's bullet hit Bowdre in the belt buckle, bounced off and wounded George Coe.

Everyone ran for safety. Roberts worked his lever gun swiftly, spraying lead at everyone he saw. He hit Middleton and Scurlock—the latter not severely—and another of his shots scraped Billy's arm. The Kid retreated to a less-exposed position.

Counting Roberts' shots, Billy knew his Winchester was empty. He dashed forward, leveling his own rifle. Roberts punched Billy in the side with the barrel of his empty Winchester, throwing the Kid's aim off. Billy withdrew. Seriously wounded, Roberts backed into Blazer's house. He took Blazer's gun, a Springfield army rifle. Barricading the door, he propped himself up against a back wall with the Springfield and prepared to fight until death.

Brewer was angry at how badly the attack had gone. He ordered some Regulators to go in after the brave Roberts, but his orders were refused. He tried to convince Dr. Blazer to talk Roberts out, but he refused. Frustrated, Brewer decided to get Roberts himself.

Billy the Kid was about eighteen years old when he became a member of the Regulators. This undated photograph shows what is thought to be the Kid near the age of eighteen. If this were actually a portrait of the outlaw, it would only be the second known image of him.

He took up a position behind a woodpile about 125 yards from the house. The door to Blazer's office (where Roberts was holed up) was standing open. Brewer aimed into the dark rectangle and fired.

The old buffalo hunter Roberts was dying, but he was not finished yet. He propped the Springfield on a mattress and aimed carefully at the puff of smoke rising from Brewer's rifle shot. The next time Dick Brewer rose to take aim, Roberts killed him with a single shot through his left eye.[8]

That did it for the Regulators. Roberts was too tough for them, and they rode away. Roberts died the next day from his original stomach wound. He and Dick Brewer were buried in the same grave.

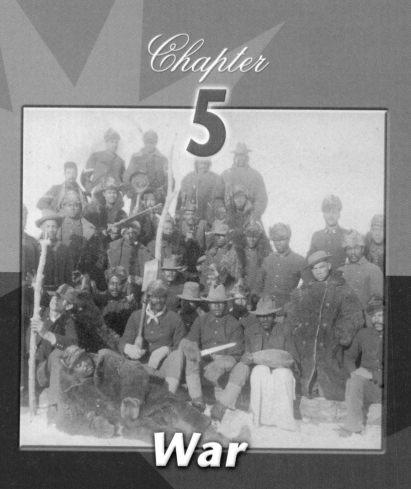

Chapter 5

War

The bloodshed in Lincoln County continued for a long time. John Tunstall, one of the leaders of the groups, was one of the first to fall. But his death did not prevent further violence; it provoked more. Alexander McSween was no leader of men, so Tunstall's foreman, Dick Brewer, organized the Regulators for their campaign of vengeance. Then Brewer was killed by Buckshot Roberts. Brewer's death provided a second chance for the gunmen in Tunstall's employ to call it quits. They did not.

The Lincoln County War Continues

Why did they keep fighting? The Regulators were not on Tunstall's payroll any more. A need for revenge should have been satisfied with the deaths of Buck Morton and Tom Hill, the men who actually killed Tunstall, or the death of Sheriff Brady, Dolan's chief enforcer. But the Regulators were not behaving like ordinary gangsters. Their war was no longer just a turf war over money, cattle, and land. It was about personal honor and manhood, as defined on the frontier in 1878. Billy the Kid and the rest had been hired to defend Tunstall and fight his enemies. They let their boss be killed, and that stained their honor. Until they paid the Dolan organization back for this insult, they would not rest.

Despite having his number-one enemy dead, Jimmy Dolan and the House were not in very good shape in the spring of 1878. Dolan had lost his court case when a Lincoln County grand jury dismissed charges of embezzlement against McSween. Jesse Evans, the bold and brutal leader of the Boys, might have been able to suppress the Regulators, but he was jailed in Fort Stanton. Dolan and his partner John H. Riley lost money and business due to the ongoing violence and court cases. By March 1878, Dolan & Co. was bankrupt. The House was closed and Dolan's assets were seized by his creditors.[1]

A new sheriff, John Copeland, was appointed to replace the slain Brady. McSween had a strong influence over him, to the extent Copeland refused to serve warrants on Billy and other leading Regulators. It was

Alexander McSween (above) had a strong influence over the new sheriff, John Copeland, which helped keep Billy the Kid and his fellow Regulators out of jail.

not as though the Iron Clads were hard to find. They were hanging around McSween's house in Lincoln for all to see. The Regulators elected Frank McNab their new captain and sat back to await the results of McSween's legal and political maneuvering.

Frank McNab did not last long as chief. At the end of April, he was ambushed by a posse of Dolan's men and killed, along with another man. Frank Coe escaped death, but was captured by the posse.

Another Gunfight

Led by former Brady deputies Billy Matthews and George Peppin, the Dolan posse rode back to Lincoln with Coe as their prisoner. They holed up in Dolan's store, even though it was closed down by bankruptcy. The next morning, April 30, Sheriff Copeland and the Regulators at McSween's house learned their enemies were in town. Billy and the rest quickly surrounded the House. George Coe fired the first shot, a long range one from a Sharps rifle. He hit one of the Dolan men in the leg.[2] After that, shooting erupted all around. The Dolan men abandoned the store, and Frank Coe walked away unscathed. For four hours, the Dolan posse and the Regulators traded fire. No one was hurt except the man George Coe hit with his first shot.

Sheriff Copeland asked the U.S. Army at Fort Stanton for help. By mid-afternoon a lieutenant and twenty cavalry troopers arrived (the cavalrymen were African Americans, the famous "buffalo soldiers"). Their arrival put an end to the fighting. The Dolan men surrendered to army custody because they feared they would be murdered if the Regulators got hold of them.

Billy's role in the "battle of Lincoln" is unclear. He did not hit anyone in the general exchange of gunfire, and, after the cavalry arrived, he slipped out of town. Another useless barrage of warrants was exchanged between McSween and Dolan, each side accusing the other of murder. Nothing came of the warrants.

A Failed Raid

Doc Scurlock was elected third chief of the Regulators. On May 15, he led a raid on a camp used by Dolan and Riley's men, who were rounding up cattle to sell to the army. Among the prisoners taken was Manuel Segovia, alias "Indian," one of the posse who killed Frank McNab. Segovia was marked for death, and he knew it. He pleaded with his captor, Francisco Trujillo, to protect him from certain death. But Trujillo could not save him. Later, Segovia tried to run for it. Billy and Jose Chavez shot him dead.[3]

The raid was a mistake. The livestock did not legally belong to Dolan, but to the man he owed money, cattle baron and New Mexico political boss Thomas B. Catron. The wealthy Catron complained to the governor and to the commander of the Army in the New Mexico Territory. Governor Axtell promptly removed Copeland as sheriff and replaced him with Brady's old deputy, George Peppin.

By this time the events in New Mexico had a wide-ranging effect. Because John Tunstall was a prominent English citizen, the British government asked U.S. Federal authorities to look into his murder. The Justice and Interior departments sent a representative, Frank Warner Angel, to investigate Tunstall's death.[4] Angel arrived in Lincoln and took sworn statements from many of those involved, including Billy Bonney.

Sheriff Copeland called on the U.S. Army to end a gunfight between the Regulators and Dolan's men. The famous "buffalo soldiers" stopped the fighting. This is a photo of the buffalo soldiers of the 25th Infantry in 1890.

Trouble for the Regulators

Meanwhile, the Regulators were in trouble. The new sheriff, Peppin, was solidly in Jimmy Dolan's camp. He gathered a large force of men, including U.S. cavalry and a band of outlaws from the Mesilla Valley, led by Jesse Evans' old friend John Kinney. The outlaws took an oath to enforce the law, becoming instant deputy sheriffs. They had more warrants for the arrest of various Regulators, including a federal warrant for Billy and the others who participated in the shootout at Blazer's Mill. Threatened by such overwhelming power, the Regulators abandoned Lincoln in mid-June, taking to the mountains to hide. Peppin's posses combed the countryside. They had several brushes with the Regulators, but were driven off time and again. Billy and his comrades used the town of San Patricio as their base, but Peppin's men eventually forced them out.

The Regulators fell back to John Chisum's ranch. Chisum was one of those celebrated men who had ruthlessly carved out an empire of cattle and land in the Southwest. Chisum was away when the Regulators arrived, but his ranch hands welcomed Billy and company, and even prepared a feast for them. Chisum had backed Tunstall and McSween with money and influence, so his people were sympathetic to the Regulators' plight.

Billy took the opportunity to renew his acquaintance with Sallie Chisum, John Chisum's sixteen-year-old niece.[5] One morning, Billy left the ranch with George and Frank Coe to buy Sallie candy at a nearby store.

John Chisum had built a prosperous cattle empire in New Mexico. His money and influence supported the Regulators, McSween, and Tunstall.

Returning, he and the Coes were chased by part of Peppin's posse. Shooting and riding, the trio managed to get back to the Chisum place. There were no casualties, and the banquet went on as planned. Reinforcements from Lincoln arrived at the Chisum ranch, but by the time they got there, Billy and the Regulators were gone.

The Federal government by this time had forbidden the U.S. Army from assisting either faction in Lincoln County.[6] That restored a certain balance to the war, but it also meant the violence would not end any time soon.

John Chisum

John Chisum (1824–1884) was born in Tennessee. He moved to Texas in 1837—after the territory won independence from Mexico—and first worked as a builder. By 1854 he had gone into the cattle business. He took over a vast stretch of land along the Pecos River. His herd grew to 100,000 heads of cattle. After the Civil War, he moved them westward into New Mexico to exploit the open spaces there. Chisum sold large amounts of beef to the U.S. Army and to mining camps in Colorado, becoming wealthy and influential in the process.

Chisum was the silent third partner of Alexander McSween and John Tunstall. He put up money and used his influence to counteract the monopoly of Dolan and Riley's House, which competed with Chisum for lucrative sales to the Army and Indian reservations. Friends and hired guns of the House, in turn, preyed on Chisum's cattle, but no one dared take on the powerful cattleman directly. Chisum had played host to John Tunstall's gunmen, since they were allies. But after the Lincoln County War ended, many of the Englishman's hired guns began rustling Chisum's plentiful cattle.

Chisum outlived his most famous nemesis, Billy the Kid, by three years. Chisum's valuable cattle empire passed to his brothers and their children.

At about this time, Billy gained a new friend. Tom O'Folliard was two years younger than Billy (about seventeen), and looked up to the veteran Regulator in every way. He became Billy's closest companion and would assist Billy in future exploits.

A Three-way Struggle

One person who was tired of running was Alexander McSween. After the shootout at the Chisum ranch, he went back to his home in Lincoln on July 14. McSween took an escort of sixty men (including Billy) with him. They occupied several buildings, including McSween's house, barricading themselves inside and taking up firing positions on rooftops.

Dolan and Peppin were in town with just forty men. They did not move until reinforcements arrived, led by none other than Jesse Evans and John Kinney. Evans had been acquitted of horse theft, and was out on bail for his alleged role in Tunstall's murder.[7] With so many violent men in town, most of the ordinary people of Lincoln fled. Four days of sniping followed without result. Sheriff Peppin wrote to the army commander, Colonel Dudley, asking for a howitzer (a short-barreled cannon) to blow up the buildings occupied by McSween and the Regulators. Under new rules from Congress, Dudley could not assist the sheriff. But when soldiers under Dudley's command

> **With so many violent men in town, most of the ordinary people of Lincoln fled.**

were fired on, probably by both sides, the colonel decided he had just cause to intervene.

On July 19, 1878, Colonel Dudley rode into Lincoln with a cavalry company, an infantry company, a twelve-pound howitzer, and a Gatling gun (a rapid-fire weapon). Though he proclaimed his neutrality in the dispute between Dolan and McSween, Colonel Dudley had his cannon pointed at one of the buildings held by the Regulators and warned everyone he would blast the place if anyone fired at his men.[8]

An unusual three-way power struggle followed. The colonel offered protection to all women and children in town, and any of the gunmen who wished to surrender. Few took him up on the offer, as appearing in the streets of Lincoln was an invitation to be shot at.

Violent End to the War

Sheriff Peppin's men next tried to storm McSween's house. They broke the windows' glass and tried to pry up the windows' sashes with knives. The defenders withdrew out of sight inside the house, firing as they went. Peppin's men poured coal oil on the wooden floor and set it on fire. Later, the sheriff's men piled sacks of tinder against an outside door and ignited it too. All the while they were under heavy fire from the Regulators. The shooting became so intense Colonel Dudley's men had to take shelter.

McSween's house was burning. The fire consumed the west side, burned across the front, and started to burn down the east end of the building. Suddenly, there

Posse Comitatus

The Posse Comitatus Act was passed by the U.S. Congress on June 16, 1878. The purpose of the law was to control the federal government's use of the military for law enforcement. Since the American Revolution, there had been strong public sentiment against the use of the military to enforce laws. The presidential election of 1876 caused a crisis that indirectly led to the Posse Comitatus Act. The Southern states, still under military occupation after the Civil War, made a deal with Northern Republicans to support the disputed presidential victory of Rutherford B. Hayes over Democrat Samuel Tilden. In return, the Republicans agreed to withdraw Federal troops from the South, where they had been enforcing various acts of the Reconstruction (especially protecting the civil rights of former African-American slaves).

The Posse Comitatus Act prohibits members of the military from enforcing state and local laws, and prevents them from acting as police officers on nonfederal property. The Act generally prohibits federal military personnel and the National Guard under federal authority from acting as law enforcement within the United States, except when authorized by the Constitution or Congress. The Coast Guard is exempt from the Act. The role of the army in the Lincoln County War was one of the first tests of the Posse Comitatus Act.

Colonel Dudley's actions led to his being removed from command at Fort Stanton. He was court-martialed for exceeding his authority. Eventually, Colonel Dudley was cleared of all charges.[9]

Colonel Dudley brought a Gatling gun into Lincoln County to intervene in the struggle between the Dolan group and the Regulators. The gun was developed during the Civil War. It was the first practical machine gun.

was an explosion. Only one room in McSween's house had not been consumed by flames—the kitchen on the northeast side. Everyone gathered there. Billy, Tom O'Folliard, and their comrades dashed outside to escape the flames. One Regulator was shot dead. Though blasted at point-blank range, Billy and his friends were not hurt.[10]

McSween was not so lucky. Driven out by smoke and fire, McSween was so heavily shot at that he retreated. McSween called out that he wanted to surrender. A Peppin deputy named Beckwith offered to take McSween prisoner, but when he stepped forward one of McSween's gunmen shot him dead. Some other deputies returned fire and McSween died, falling across Beckwith's body.[11]

The five-day battle soon ended. Besides McSween, three Regulators died. Peppin's men were so happy to have killed the troublesome lawyer they forced McSween's servants to play fiddles while they drank and danced around McSween's corpse.[12]

The Lincoln County War was over. Billy the Kid was now without a cause.

6

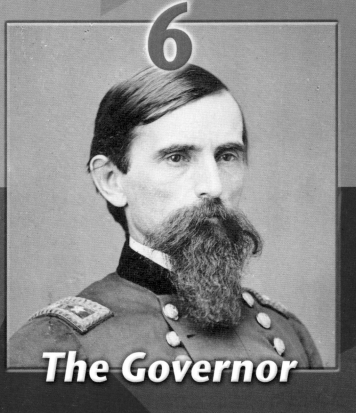

The Governor

Samuel Axtell, governor of the New Mexico Territory during the Lincoln County War, had come to the end of his service. He had accepted a bribe from Jimmy Dolan, called a "loan" and always bowed to the wishes of powerful cattle barons like Thomas Catron.[1] Worst of all, he had never been able to stop the violence in Lincoln County. When Frank Angel arrived in May 1878 to investigate the conflict, he found ample evidence of the governor's corruption, ineptitude, and general failure to govern.

Angel's report to President Rutherford B. Hayes resulted in Axtell being removed from office.

A New Governor

In Axtell's place, President Hayes appointed General Lew Wallace, a man with much and varied experience. He had been a general in the Union Army during the Civil War. He served on the court-martial that tried the conspirators in the assassination of President Abraham Lincoln. He also presided over the only war crimes trial after the war: Henry Wirtz, Confederate commandant of the Andersonville prisoner of war camp, was tried, convicted, and executed for the brutal way the camp was run.

Back home in Indiana, Wallace practiced law and wrote novels. His first book, *Fair God*, was published in 1873.[2] At the time of the Lincoln County War, he was working on his greatest story, *Ben Hur*. Lawyer, general, novelist, Lew Wallace was also a romantic. He liked grand statements and even grander gestures. He also had a reputation for honesty, so President Hayes dispatched him to New Mexico to bring peace to the region.

Upon arrival, Wallace reviewed the situation and called for a cease-fire by all parties. He offered amnesty to everyone involved in the war—everyone except those already under criminal indictment. Billy was still wanted in Arizona for Windy Cahill's murder, and he was also wanted in Sheriff Brady's death, so Wallace's amnesty was no good to him.

President Rutherford B. Hayes appointed General Lew Wallace, pictured here, as governor of the New Mexico Territory.

Next, Wallace removed some of the more obvious partisans from public office. Dolan loyalist Sheriff Peppin was replaced by George Kimbrell, a one-time scout for the army.

A "Peaceful" Meeting

In the new spirit of peace, a meeting was arranged between the hard-core Regulators and Jimmy Dolan. On February 18, 1879, Billy the Kid went to Lincoln with Tom O'Folliard, Doc Scurlock, and two other men. Meeting them were Dolan and some of his toughest gunmen: Jesse Evans, Billy Matthews, Edgar Walz, and Billy Campbell. The two parties stood on either side of a road and talked about making peace. Evans almost ruined the whole meeting by declaring Billy ought to be killed on the spot, but the two sides finally agreed to a cease-fire. They also agreed not to testify against each other, should any of them come to trial.[3]

The two parties began drinking—except Billy Bonney—to seal their pact. Once they were drunk, they went looking for trouble. They ran into a lawyer named Houston Chapman, who worked for Alexander McSween's widow. The drunken

> **Evans almost ruined the whole meeting by declaring Billy ought to be killed on the spot . . .**

gunmen badgered and bullied Chapman, demanding he dance a jig for them. When he refused, he was promptly shot dead by Dolan and Campbell.

As the only sober one in the group, Billy knew there was no covering up the murder of Chapman. He found a reason to depart, taking the loyal O'Folliard with him.

Governor Wallace came to Lincoln County to find out what was going on and to uncover who was responsible for Chapman's death. He arrived in Lincoln in early March and ordered the lawman in Lincoln to go after Chapman's killers. Wallace also engineered the removal of Colonel Dudley, the commander of Fort Stanton. His replacement, Captain Henry Carroll, headed an investigation into who the worst culprits of the war were, and who might be eligible for amnesty. During one military sweep several notorious characters were detained. Jimmy Dolan was caught, along with Jesse Evans, Billy Campbell, and Billy Matthews.[4] They were put in the stockade at Fort Stanton.

Billy's Letters to the Governor

Captain Carroll hunted Regulators, too. His troopers rounded up quite a few, but missed the elusive Billy. Still, the vigorous campaign must have impressed the Kid, and he decided not to wait to be arrested. Billy wrote the first of several letters to Governor Wallace on March 13, 1879. He wrote, in part:

> *I was present when Mr. Chapman was murdered and know who did it. If it is arranged so that I could appear at court, I could give the desired information, but I have indictments against me for things that happened in the late Lincoln County War, and am afraid to give up because my enemies would kill me. . . . If it is in your power to annul these indictments, I hope you will do so, so as to give me a chance to explain.*[5]

Wallace agreed to meet the young outlaw at Justice Wilson's house on the night of March 17. Billy entered cautiously, a rifle in one hand and a pistol in the other. Wallace held out his hand and invited Billy in. He asked Billy to testify in court about who killed Houston Chapman.

Billy refused, saying that if he spoke in open court, the accused men, or their friends, would surely kill him. Governor Wallace countered that he would stage a fake arrest for Billy. While in protective custody he would be safe from Dolan and his cronies.

Billy then agreed. Even though Campbell and Evans soon escaped from their army prison, Billy and Tom

This letter from Governor Lew Wallace to Billy the Kid (W. H. Bonney), was written on March 15, 1879. Billy the Kid and the governor exchanged several letters.

O'Folliard allowed themselves to be quietly arrested on March 21 by Sheriff Kimbrell and his posse. They were held at a house in Lincoln under guard.

Wallace was amused by the reaction of many residents of Lincoln to Billy's presence. They stood outside his window and sang to him, played music, and generally made him feel welcome. Compared to Evans or Dolan, Billy was well liked, even respected by many people in the community. The governor was less impressed with the young outlaw. In a letter to Secretary of the Interior Carl Schurz, Wallace referred to Billy as "a precious specimen."[6]

Wallace referred to Billy as "a precious specimen."

While under arrest, Billy wrote several letters to the governor, detailing what he knew about crime in New Mexico. He described outlaws' habits, secret trails, and personalities. Just what Billy thought he was accomplishing by doing this is not clear. Was he trying to impress a worldly older man with his knowledge of local crime? Or was he pushing the governor to live up to his promise to pardon Billy for his past deeds?

Lew Wallace was not clear in his own mind about what he wanted to do with Billy Bonney. He had given his word to help the Kid, but what he meant and what Billy wanted proved to be entirely different.

Billy wanted a pardon. As governor, Wallace could have pardoned him at any time. Wallace thought Billy should be exempt from prosecution—a subtle but very different concept. By pardoning the young outlaw, Wallace would have made Billy immune to prosecution for all his past deeds. Exempting him merely meant the governor had no intention of bringing Billy to justice. Wallace soon returned to Santa Fe, leaving Billy in the hands of William L. Rynerson, the district attorney of Lincoln County. Rynerson was a Dolan man, and he was not going to let the Kid get away.

Testimony in Court

A grand jury was convened to look into the death of Houston Chapman. As promised, Billy took the stand and testified that Dolan and Billy Campbell had killed the hapless lawyer. Jesse Evans was the instigator of the deed, Billy declared, by his drunken demand that Chapman dance for them. The grand jury indicted all three men.

If Billy thought he would walk out of custody a free man after testifying, he was wrong. Rynerson was determined that Billy would pay for his acts against the Dolan faction. Meanwhile, the trial of Jimmy Dolan was moved out of Lincoln. As a result, Dolan was acquitted of murder and passed into quiet retirement.[7] One of the chief instigators of the Lincoln County War, Dolan spent the rest of his life in Lincoln County, dying in 1898. He spent time in the Territorial Senate and, ironically, eventually purchased all the land once owned by John Tunstall.[8] Rynerson went on preparing a case against Billy that would put a noose around his neck.

> **If Billy thought he would walk out of custody a free man after testifying, he was wrong.**

Billy and Doc Scurlock were not in jail, although technically under arrest. Everyone in Lincoln knew the Kid would run for it if he got the chance. Charges in federal district court for the murder of Buckshot Roberts loomed over Billy too. (It was claimed that Roberts died on U.S. government property, making his death a federal case.) When it became clear he was going to be jailed for real, Billy decided to clear out of town. With Governor Wallace's hollow promises still rankling, Billy and Doc Scurlock rode out of Lincoln on June 17, 1879.

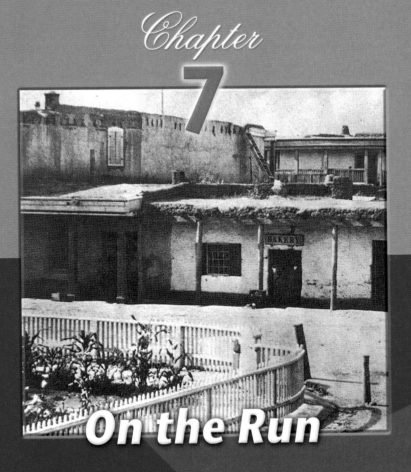

BAKERY

On the Run

Billy Bonney did not run far. He made it to Las Vegas—not the modern city in Nevada, but Las Vegas, New Mexico, seventy-five miles from Sante Fe—where he lived openly, supporting himself by gambling. He actually lived at a former army post called Fort Sumner, about one hundred miles from Las Vegas.[1] There was no law at Fort Sumner, as the sheriff of San Miguel County was busy keeping the peace in the booming railroad center at Las Vegas. For the rest of his life, the Fort Sumner area would be Billy's home.

Gambling

Many settlers in the American West were ardent gamblers. From the earliest days, when lone trappers and mountain men played games of chance with local American Indians, the frontier was dotted with gambling halls, saloons, and gaming parlors. Cattle, gold, and greenbacks were wagered on a single turn of a card or throw of the dice. Losing could mean ruin, suicide, or violence against the winner.

Poker was popular, and in more settled towns, games like roulette were common. One of the most popular western games of chance, not played much today, was faro. The name is derived from Pharaoh, as the rulers of Ancient Egypt were called. French-made playing cards in the early nineteenth century often had Egyptian designs. The card game took its name from the decoration.[2] Players bet against the bank (the dealer), wagering on which cards of the thirteen in each suit would turn up.[3]

Billy probably played poker. It was easier to come and go, keep your own hours, buy in or cash out of a floating poker game than to manage a game like faro or roulette. Whatever his game of choice, Billy does not seem to have been particularly successful at it, as time and again he turned to a pursuit he knew well: rustling cattle. Posing as a gambler did give Billy a "profession," and served as a cover for his more overtly criminal activities.

Fort Sumner

The local people of Fort Sumner were mostly Latino sheepherders. Billy had always gotten along well with Latinos. He spoke their language and respected their ways, and they were not part of the Anglo power structure, which was centered around the cattle or mining industries. Billy needed friends. Many of his old Regulator comrades had left the territory. The Coe cousins had departed for Colorado. They tried to convince Billy to go with them, but he refused. Doc Scurlock went to Texas. Henry Brown ended up in

After clearing out of Lincoln, Billy the Kid went to Fort Sumner, New Mexico.

Kansas, working as a town marshal. He built a very respectable life there as a law officer until he attempted to rob a bank in a nearby town. The robbery failed, and Brown was gunned down trying to escape the vigilantes who had caught him.[4]

Gambling was not a sure enough source of income for Billy, so he cast about for ways to stir up some cash. Rustling was lucrative enough for Billy to acquire a new circle of colleagues. Besides the ever-loyal Tom O'Folliard and Charlie Bowdre from his Lincoln County days, Billy worked with Dave Rudabaugh, Tom Pickett, and Billy Wilson. Rumor had it that his true love, Paulita Maxwell, lived near Fort Sumner. Paulita was the sister of Pete Maxwell, who owned a sizable ranch. Later in life, Paulita would deny being Billy's lover. She said he had many girlfriends from the Latino families around Fort Sumner. However, there was an undeniable link between her and Billy, a link that would have powerful consequences.[5]

As 1880 began, Billy enjoyed his widespread reputation as a dashing outlaw—bold, fearless, but with a likeable streak that differentiated him from ruthless killers like Jesse James. (There is a legend Billy and Jesse James met in 1879, at a hot springs near Las Vegas. This has never been proven.) He was only twenty years old, but he had been an outlaw and gunslinger for several hard years, seeing more action and escaping more danger than most men encountered in a lifetime. Nevertheless, his youth and disarming appearance still fooled people.

A portrait of Jesse James taken around 1864. There is a legend that Billy the Kid met Jesse James in 1879, but there is no proof to support this theory.

"A Game of Two"

Early in 1880, Billy was in Hargrove's saloon in Fort Sumner, buying drinks for some of John Chisum's cowboys. A man named Joe "Texas Red" Grant, already drunk, began to insult the Kid and made threats. He was not impressed with the slender youth who avoided liquor, and said so. Grant took a revolver from one of the Chisum cowboys and stuck it in his own holster. It had a set of fancy pearl grips. Still friendly, Billy asked to see the gun. Grant handed it to him. Noting three rounds out of six had already been fired, Billy rotated the cylinder so that an empty, fired case would come up the next time the revolver was cocked. Grant apparently did not notice what Billy had done. The Kid gave him back the gun.

> **Whirling, Billy put three shots in Red Grant's face, killing him instantly.**

Later, Grant quarreled with Billy again. When Billy got up to leave, he heard the click of a hammer falling and knew Grant had tried to shoot him in the back. Whirling, Billy put three shots in Red Grant's face, killing him instantly.[6]

Though similar to the incident with Windy Cahill years ago in Arizona, this time Billy was prepared for the worst. When asked about Grant's death, Billy said, "It was a game of two and I got there first."[7]

After killing Grant, Billy sent word to John Chisum, claiming the cattle baron owed him back wages for his work with the late Alexander McSween. Chisum denied he owed Billy any money. He had no contract with Billy

Billy the Kid shoots Joe "Texas Red" Grant after Grant had tried to shoot Billy in the back.

and therefore owed him nothing. As a result of this exchange, Billy began rustling Chisum's plentiful cattle.[8]

The Outlaw Lifestyle

Billy's life after the Lincoln County War had a certain rhythm. He and his friends would collect cattle from the big herds and corral them in a rock-lined hollow known as Los Portales ("The Porches"). Once they had a good number of animals on hand, they would drive them to market. Their best customers were the U.S. Army at Fort Stanton, and the American Indian agents buying beef for the Apache reservation. The usual price for stolen cattle was twelve dollars a head. A broker could then resell them to the Army or the American Indian agency for twice that amount, no questions asked.[9] That was good money all around. The only ones unhappy with this arrangement were the big ranchers who were losing cattle and sales to the rustlers.

In 1879, gold was discovered at White Oaks, forty-five miles northwest of Lincoln. In no time the mining camp exploded into a boomtown, with many saloons and gambling halls opened to exploit the miners' success. Billy spent a good deal of time in White Oaks in 1880, gambling and peddling stolen cattle.

Despite what newspapers and gossip said about Billy at this time, he was not the boss of an outlaw gang like Jesse Evans had been leader of the Boys. He and his friends combined for specific jobs, then separated to pursue other interests. Billy's Fort Sumner associates were a mixed lot. There were hardened crooks like Dave

Rudabaugh, a longtime robber and killer. Billy Wilson was younger than Billy Bonney by two years, but while the Kid was lighthearted, Wilson was inclined to be somber. Tom Pickett had been a lawman in Las Vegas. He was diligent enough at his job to anger many local criminals. When they conspired to kill him, Pickett fled to Fort Sumner. He found his way into Billy's circle out of sheer necessity.

If Billy was not an outlaw gang leader, his enemies liked to describe him as one. By picking on powerful men like John Chisum, Billy insured his name would never fade from wanted posters or warrants. Every act of rustling from Las Vegas to the Texas panhandle was ascribed to outlaw gangs, of which Billy the Kid's was the best known.

Hunting Down Billy the Kid

In 1880, Texas cattle barons formed the Panhandle Stock Association (PSA). They hired "stock detectives" to track down notorious rustlers. Stock detectives were as varied as the outlaws they hunted. Some were honest, methodical men. Others were just hired killers. Agents hired by the PSA traced stolen cows to White Oaks, New Mexico, where they were told the animals had been brought in by Billy Bonney. In response, the PSA organized a posse of their own. Their mission was to track down and finish Billy the Kid.[10]

Worse, the U.S. government was on Billy's trail. The Treasury Department had reports of counterfeit money being passed in Lincoln and White Oaks. A special undercover agent was sent to New Mexico to investigate. His name was Azariah F. Wild, and he found evidence that some of Billy's colleagues were passing fake bills around White Oaks and Fort Sumner. Wild found that most of the rustling gangs were circulating bad money, Billy included. No local lawman would move against Billy or his friends. They were either afraid of the outlaws or good friends with them. Wild's report on the corrupt state of New Mexico law enforcement surprised no one, but he was able to get things done. He recruited federal deputies among the men who hated Billy—former Dolan gunmen Bob Olinger and John Hurley, who had been in Sheriff Peppin's posse during the fight that killed Alexander McSween. Wild recruited up to forty others for service against the outlaws.

> He set about replacing the lax Sheriff Kimbrell with a man who would chase Billy to the ends of the earth if necessary.

John Chisum, eager to be rid of Billy, lent his help. He set about replacing the lax Sheriff Kimbrell with a man who would chase Billy to the ends of the earth if necessary. A good candidate appeared in the form of Pat Garrett.

Sheriff Pat Garrett

Garrett was born in 1850. Like Henry Brown and Buckshot Roberts, he was a former buffalo hunter. He had come to New Mexico in 1878 and held a few jobs, including bartender at Beaver Smith's saloon. Garrett was six-feet, six-inches tall—the tallest man around. He was known to be cool, brave, and tough. Like Billy, he got along well with the Latino community (he married twice, both times to Latina women).[11] They called him "Juan Largo," Long John. When the election of 1880 approached, Chisum and Joseph Lea convinced Garrett to move to Roswell, New Mexico, and run for sheriff of Lincoln County.

Billy had known Pat Garrett casually since 1878. Later, there were rumors that Garrett had ridden with Billy on outlaw forays. This is not true. Billy wanted George Kimbrell as sheriff because of the tolerant way he had treated Billy since the end of the war. Unfortunately for Billy the Kid, Garrett won the office in November by an almost two-to-one margin.[12]

By the end of 1880, Billy was the subject of two major manhunts. The PSA stock detectives were after him, and Treasury Agent Wild also wanted him. Wild set Pat Garrett on Billy's tail, and "Juan Largo" was not a man to give up easily.

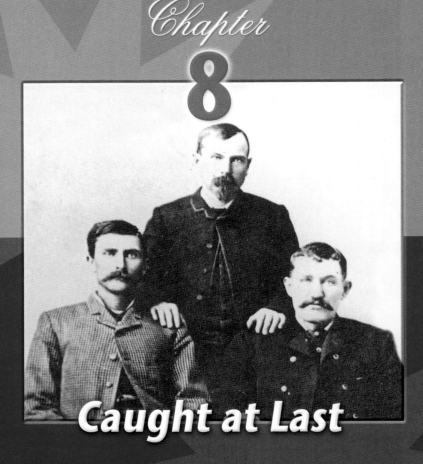

Caught at Last

E ven as the wheels of justice turned, Billy
Bonney made another attempt to end his
criminal career. He wrote letters to Ira Leonard, an
attorney working for Governor Lew Wallace, trying
to cut a new deal for amnesty. At this point, counterfeiting had been added to the list of his crimes. Billy
offered to reveal what he knew about the fake
money if Leonard and the governor would protect
him from federal prosecution. Leonard consulted
with Secret Service agent Wild, but nothing came of

their negotiations. Billy wanted immunity from all legal action, which neither Leonard nor Wild could honestly guarantee. The lawyer and the federal agent were also at odds over how to proceed against the outlaws. Like his attempt to make a deal with Wallace, Billy came away empty-handed, and so did the lawmen.

White Oaks was no longer safe for Billy and his pals. Their casual thievery and constant intimidation of the locals turned the town against them. Informers turned up, ready to report to the lawmen or the PSA detectives on Billy's doings. On November 8, 1880, a nine-man posse caught the outlaws camping at Coyote Springs. In a brisk shootout, Billy's horse was killed. He and Billy Wilson had to escape on foot, while Rudabaugh and the rest scattered. In spite of this clear evidence of local hostility, Billy remained near White Oaks. Five days later, while resting at the Greathouse ranch, the outlaws were surrounded by an even larger posse. The Kid laughed when ordered to surrender.[1]

Killing an Unarmed Man

A local blacksmith named Carlyle went in to talk to the rustlers. Carlyle knew Billy Wilson, and believed he could talk the young man out without any trouble. Unfortunately the outlaws, except for the Kid, had been drinking heavily and, in a mean mood, they refused to let Carlyle leave. They plied the unhappy blacksmith with whiskey, getting him drunk too. A tense couple of hours passed, with everyone inside the ranch growing more and more irrational. Fearing for his life, Carlyle

Cattle rustlers hide their faces with masks in this 1880 photograph taken in Nebraska. Billy the Kid made his money rustling cattle. Billy and his friends' constant thievery turned the town of White Oaks against them.

decided to bolt. He went through a window to escape and was killed by a hail of shots from inside and outside the house.[2]

The posse abandoned the siege. They were not equipped for a long standoff, and Carlyle's death shocked them. Both sides blamed the other for the blacksmith's death, but it was widely reported that Billy was the principal shooter, taking deliberate aim at the unarmed, fleeing man. If true, this was his most reprehensible killing. Carlyle was no bully, picking on Billy, or trying to shoot him in the back like Grant. He was not an armed (but unsuspecting) lawman like Sheriff Brady. Billy could not even claim drunkenness as a excuse because he did not drink.

The murder of Jimmy Carlyle ended whatever welcome Billy and his friends enjoyed around White Oaks. Local papers began trumpeting his deeds—some real, some imaginary—elevating the twenty-year-old Kid to being boss of a gang of forty to fifty desperadoes who stole whatever they wanted and killed anyone who got in their way. These stories began to sound like the deeds of Jesse Evans' old gang, the Boys. The difference was that the Boys existed, whereas Billy's supposed gang never did. He committed many crimes, but he was no mastermind leading an army of outlaws. This negative publicity had two serious effects. First, it made Billy famous, although in a very sinister way. Second, it made it impossible for Governor Wallace to extend any kind of clemency to the Kid. The public would have been outraged if the governor had shown any mercy to the "desperate cuss" who killed without mercy.[3]

Claiming Innocence

Billy tried to change the governor's mind. He wrote again to Wallace, claiming he was nowhere near White Oaks when Carlyle was murdered. He declared, "I have been at [Fort] Sumner since I left Lincoln making my living gambling."[4] The trigger-happy posse at Greathouse's ranch killed Carlyle, he said. Billy blamed all his bad press on John Chisum. Having made an enemy of the great cattle baron, Chisum was using his influence to blacken Billy's name and get him killed or caught.

Billy's claims of innocence did not impress the governor. He passed the outlaw's letters to the newspapers, which mocked Billy's obvious lie about not being around White Oaks.

As Billy's infamy grew, more men turned out to ride in Pat Garrett's posses. Sometimes two hundred men were marshaled in several groups, scouring the countryside for Billy and his comrades. Even though Billy persisted in staying in the Fort Sumner area, no one could quite lay hands on him. He hid out in the hills, changing camps constantly so as not to be found. Other times he sought refuge with friends, such as Latino sheepherders in the area.

Surprisingly, Billy responded to a census taker for the 1880 U.S. census. He was living with Charlie Bowdre, he said, and gave his age as twenty-five. Billy listed his profession as "cattle worker."[5] Actually, Billy was still twenty-one when the census data was taken. He had no fixed address, but circulated among congenial Anglo ranches and Latino friends.

Many men joined Pat Garrett in hunting for Billy the Kid. These three lawmen include Garrett (left), James Brent (center), and John Poe.

Garrett Closing In On the Kid

In November, a large raid on Fort Sumner organized by Garrett and agent Wild just missed Billy, who still operated near White Oaks. Feeling the pressure, the Kid and his closest associates—Rudabaugh, O'Folliard, Billy Wilson, and Tom Pickett—decided to get out of Fort Sumner and maybe out of New Mexico for good. They even wrote to various officials, telling them they planned to get out. Pat Garrett was not fooled. He vowed to keep after the outlaws until he caught them, dead or alive.

Pat Garrett meant every word. Though it was December, and snow was falling, he pushed on with a small posse of thirteen men. Near Fort Sumner, Garrett got word his quarry was nearby. He sent a boy named Jose Roibal ahead to find out where the outlaws were hiding. Roibal was caught by O'Folliard and Pickett. They let him go when they believed his story that he was a sheepherder searching for stray animals. Roibal passed word to Garrett, who brought his men to Fort Sumner to trap the outlaws.[6]

On the morning of December 18, Garrett openly entered the town square at Fort Sumner. Word got back to Billy, who was at the Wilcox ranch, twelve miles east of Fort Sumner. Garrett sent a note to rancher Wilcox, asking for his help in rounding up the outlaws. Billy and company saw the note. They laughed at it because they thought Garrett's request for help meant he was afraid to tackle the outlaws even with a small posse behind him. They decided to ride to Fort Sumner themselves and drive Garrett off.[7]

Garrett sensed they would come. He and the posse waited in comfort in Fort Sumner while snow fell. Upon hearing horses approach, Garrett summoned his men to battle. He knew that only the outlaws would be out in this weather.

Trapped

As the rustlers neared the house where the posse was sheltering, Billy sensed danger. He was leading the group, but suddenly turned back to borrow some chewing tobacco from a rider farther back in line. That left O'Folliard and Pickett at the head of the band. When the outlaws were near the porch, Garrett, hidden from sight, shouted "Halt!" O'Folliard went for his gun, but Garrett and one of his deputies fired first. O'Folliard tried to gallop away, but he was fatally wounded. He rode slowly back toward the waiting lawmen. He pleaded with the lawmen to kill him outright. Garrett refused. O'Folliard died less than an hour later.[8]

The outlaws fled in disorder, startled by the violent response of the posse and disheartened by the death of O'Folliard. Garrett pursued them deliberately, letting fear and the harsh winter weather take some of the fight out of the usually high-spirited Billy. When he caught up with Billy and the rest at Stinking Springs on December 23, another exchange of gunfire killed outlaw Charlie Bowdre. Billy and his companions surrendered. It looked like the end of an infamous gang.

JAMES W. BELL
DEPUTY SHERIFF
BORN—1853—DIED APRIL 28.1881
MURDERED BY WILLIAM BONNEY
A.K.A. "BILLY THE KID"
DURING HIS ESCAPE FROM THE
LINCOLN COUNTY JAIL.
LINCOLN, N. M.

Follow Me No Longer

One of the first things Billy did upon arrival in Las Vegas was grant an interview to the town paper, the *Gazette*. The interview was printed on December 28, 1880. In it the reporter described the curious crowds that surrounded the jail trying to get a glimpse of the infamous prisoners. Some people went out of their way to be kind to the outlaws. Mike Cosgrove, a mailman who casually knew Billy and his friends, brought each man a new suit in jail, "to see the boys go away in style."[1]

Getting to Know the Outlaw

The men had to be unshackled by a blacksmith so they could don their new clothes. Billy was chained to Billy Wilson, who was downcast by their capture. In contrast, the Kid was outgoing—laughing, cracking jokes, and generally being pleasant, in spite of his serious predicament and the recent deaths of two of his best friends, Tom O'Folliard and Charlie Bowdre.

"You appear to take it easy," the *Gazette* reporter said.

"Yes! What's the use of looking on the gloomy side of everything?" the Kid replied.[2]

He enjoyed the attention of the crowd and told the reporter he hoped the people would see he was a man and not a wild animal, as he was portrayed in some publications. This is the *Gazette*'s description of Billy at this time:

> *He did look human, indeed, but there was nothing very mannish about his appearance, for he looked and acted a mere boy. He is about five feet eight or nine inches tall, slightly built and lithe, weighing about 140; a frank and open countenance, looking like a school boy, with the traditional silky fuzz on his upper lip; clear blue eyes, with a roguish snap about them; light hair and complexion. He is, in all, quite a handsome fellow, the imperfection being two prominent front teeth, slighting protruding like squirrels' teeth, and he has agreeable and winning ways.[3]*

The story quoted Billy at length about how he was maligned by the press and his enemies, that he did not commit a fraction of the offenses laid at his door, and so on. He said Pat Garrett was simply lucky to have caught them, though he did credit the sheriff for shooting the horse that blocked the only way out.

Not everyone was charmed by the Kid. When the outlaws were being transferred to Santa Fe, an angry crowd formed at the train station. The mob was there mainly to protest Dave Rudabaugh being sent away to stand trial in Santa Fe. The brutal Rudabaugh was hated in Las Vegas. Garrett and his deputies faced down the crowd, but the situation grew uglier by the minute. Garrett declared he would give Billy a gun to defend himself if the mob attacked, but Billy read their temper more accurately.[4] He told Garrett the mob would not fight, and they didn't. Miguel Otero, a leader in the Latino community, addressed the crowd. While they were distracted, one of Garrett's deputies got the train moving.

> "Yes! What's the use of looking on the gloomy side of everything?"

In the Santa Fe Jail

Among the guards on the train was Bob Olinger, one of Garrett's deputies who had been in the posse at Stinking Springs. While some of the men escorting the outlaws to Santa Fe were clearly impressed with the Kid, Olinger was not, and said so. Olinger's hostility stemmed from the fact that his good friend Bob Beckwith had been shot in Lincoln the day Alexander McSween was killed. Olinger blamed the Regulators, and Billy in particular, for his friend's death.

Billy spent three months in the Santa Fe jail. He tried to write to Governor Wallace again, only to find the governor was back East enjoying the acclaim that followed publication of his novel *Ben Hur.* In his place, Wallace appointed W. G. Ritch as acting governor. Ritch was a crony of former Governor Axtell, a Dolan man and certainly no friend of Billy Bonney. His letters to the acting governor went unheeded.

Undaunted, Billy the Kid, Rudabaugh, and Wilson tried to tunnel their way out of jail. They made considerable progress until an informer among the prisoners gave the plan away. The outlaws were shackled again and constantly watched.

Billy the Kid faced counterfeiting charges in Mesilla, as did Billy Wilson. In addition, there were multiple federal and local indictments, including the murder of Buckshot Roberts and Sheriff Brady. The Kid's appointed defender, Ira Leonard, successfully argued against the federal murder charge in the case of Buckshot Roberts. The government claimed jurisdiction in the Roberts case because Blazer's Mill stood on a federal American Indian reservation. Leonard proved Blazer's house existed before the reservation had been established, and therefore the land was private, not government property. The federal murder indictment was dismissed on April 6, 1881.[5]

After his capture, Billy the Kid spent three months in the Santa Fe jail. This is an illustration of a street near the Plaza in Santa Fe in the late nineteenth century.

On Trial for Murder

Billy the Kid's trial for the murder of Sheriff Brady followed two days later. Records of this trial are strangely hard to find. The chief witness against Billy was former deputy Billy Matthews, who was present at the ambush and had returned fire, wounding the Kid in the leg. Other witnesses from Lincoln were called, but the substance of their testimony has not been preserved. It must have been convincing, for the jury on April 13 brought in a verdict of guilty of murder in the first degree.

Judge Bristol sentenced Billy to death by hanging. The sentence was to be carried out on May 13, one month after the verdict.[6]

A reporter caught up with Governor Wallace soon after and asked him if he would pardon the Kid. Wallace answered that he could not imagine why Billy should expect mercy when he had already destroyed his chance for clemency by committing so many new crimes after the Lincoln County War had ended. Nevertheless, Billy felt victimized. Of all the gunmen and corrupt politicians involved in the Lincoln County War, he was the only convicted in a court of law.

Going Back to Lincoln

Billy was put in a wagon in Mesilla for the journey back to Lincoln on the night of April 16. He had a heavy guard of seven men. Three of them were old-time enemies of the Kid: Billy Matthews, Sheriff Brady's deputy; John

Kinney, once Jesse Evans' partner in one of the biggest rustling operations in the territory; and Bob Olinger, who held a deadly grudge against Billy. That these three would be allowed to escort Billy Bonney to jail said a lot about the lingering corruption still common in New Mexico.

> "Lincoln County did not then have a jail that would hold a cripple."

Olinger was one of the many glowering bullies who appear in Billy's history. Described as six feet tall and two hundred pounds of muscle, Olinger gloated over Billy's impending fate. On the ride to Lincoln, Olinger sat across from the Kid with a loaded shotgun. Billy was manacled and surrounded by alert guards. He talked a lot on the trip (which took five days), but he made no move to escape. He understood it would not take much to inspire his guards to shoot him dead.

Nothing much happened on the long journey. On April 21, Pat Garrett met the wagon and officially took charge of Billy on behalf of Lincoln County. Garrett assigned two deputies to guard the Kid: J. W. Bell and Bob Olinger.

"Lincoln County did not then have a jail that would hold a cripple," wrote Garrett in his memoir, so Billy was held on the second floor of a converted store building.[7] Ironically, this was the former Dolan & Co. store, the infamous "House." The county had bought the empty building for public use while a real jail was under construction. Billy the Kid was kept on the upper floor, away from less notorious prisoners who were held on the ground floor. Access to the second floor could only be had by an outside staircase.

While Billy was there, he tried to defend or evade responsibility for any of his crimes. Garrett replied that the Kid should hang, if only for the murder of Carlyle, the innocent, unarmed blacksmith shot in the back as he tried to flee.[8]

When the other men were not around, Billy tried to charm Deputy Bell, who had no past history in Lincoln like Olinger. Bell was a decent man, and he treated his prisoner properly and with respect. Unfortunately, he stood between Billy and freedom, and when the time came, Bell's life did not matter as much to Billy as his liberty.

This is the Lincoln County Courthouse where Billy was held as a prisoner awaiting his execution.

Escape

On the evening of April 28, Bob Olinger paraded the county prisoners across the street for dinner. This left Bell alone with Billy on the second floor of the store building. Pat Garrett was away, collecting county taxes.

Billy asked Bell to take him to the latrine. This was downstairs in the back corral. When they were going back upstairs, Billy was in front of the deputy. He suddenly dashed ahead. What exactly happened next is disputed. Billy claimed that he slipped the manacles off his slender wrists and used the heavy chain to strike Bell. He grabbed Bell's revolver. The deputy tried to run for help, and Billy shot him dead.

> **Just then, a voice from above called down, "Hello, Bob." When Olinger looked up, Billy let him have it with both barrels in the face and chest.**

Pat Garrett later claimed that Billy got a gun from the store of weapons in a locked closet on the second floor of the store. Another version says a friend hid a gun in the latrine for Billy.[9]

The building caretaker, Gottfried Gauss, saw Bell fall dead. He shouted for help. In the meantime, Billy went to Garrett's office and helped himself to Bob Olinger's 10-gauge shotgun. He went to the second floor window overlooking the street and waited.

Olinger had heard the shots that killed Bell and started back to the jail. Gauss warned him Billy had killed the deputy. Just then, a voice from above called

Two re-enactors perform "The Last Escape of Billy the Kid," in Lincoln, New Mexico, as part of the town's annual Old Lincoln Days celebration. These re-enactors are depicting Billy the Kid's murder of Bob Olinger during his escape.

How Many Men Did Billy Kill?

Billy the Kid died at age twenty-one. The legend grew up after he died that he had killed twenty-one men, one victim for every year of his life.

Billy's exact toll cannot be determined. He took part in several huge gun battles in which opponents died, but it cannot be proven if he was personally responsible for any of the deaths. One analysis of Billy's career as an outlaw found he definitely killed four men, participated in a total of sixteen gunfights, and had a hand in the deaths of five others—quite a toll, but a long way from a notch for every year.[10]

down, "Hello, Bob." When Olinger looked up, Billy let him have it with both barrels in the face and chest.

Smashing the shotgun over the railing, Billy threw the pieces on Olinger's body, crying, "Take it, damn you, you won't follow me any more with that gun!"[11]

With both lawmen dead, Billy was in no hurry. He ordered the elderly Gauss to bring him a tool so he could break the shackles on his legs. While he worked on his irons, Billy ordered Gauss to bring him a horse. Arming himself with a Winchester rifle and two pistols, Billy sat by the window, keeping watch on the street while he worked to free his legs. When he was free, he

This is the grave of Deputy Sheriff J. W. Bell, the man Billy the Kid killed in order to escape from Lincoln before his execution.

was reported to have capered around the second-floor balcony, laughing and shouting.

An hour passed since Bell was shot and Billy still had not left town. A few curious heads poked out to see what was going on, but as word spread of what had happened, no one dared interfere with Billy the Kid.

With one leg still chained, Billy got on a stolen horse and rode out of Lincoln for the last time.

Chapter

10

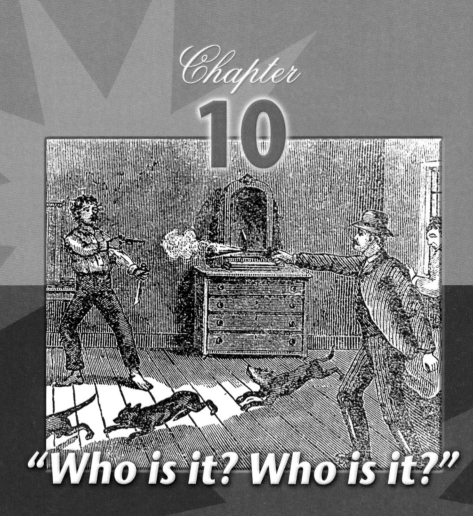

"Who is it? Who is it?"

B illy made his way to Las Tablas, to the home of Yginio Salazar, an old friend from the Lincoln County War. Salazar let the outlaw stay three days, dining at his house but spending his nights in secret camps in the surrounding hills. One night the horse he stole broke free and ran back to Lincoln. Billy stole another horse in Las Tablas and moved on. He went to the Penasco River region to find another old acquaintance, John Meadows, who urged the

Kid to go to Mexico, out of reach of Agent Wild, Governor Wallace, and Pat Garrett.

Billy was not sure. He said he was thinking of making his way back to Fort Sumner.

"Sure as you do," Meadows replied, "Garrett will get you."[1]

Returning to Fort Sumner

The Kid assured Meadows that would not happen. He had lots of friends around Fort Sumner. There, he could get money to pay his way south to Mexico, he explained. The next day Billy departed for Fort Sumner. On the way his second stolen horse bolted, leaving Billy to continue on foot. He eventually reached Fort Sumner on May 7, 1881.

He promptly stole a third horse, which alerted local lawmen. Even so, Billy lingered at Fort Sumner, bunking with friendly sheepherders, and even attending dances in town. His string of girlfriends welcomed him, for he was just as charming and more infamous than ever.

The murder of two deputies and his brazen escape further tarnished Billy's reputation. As the territory's newspapers ranted about the cold-blooded killer in their midst, one of Billy's opponents quit the field. Lew Wallace had been offered the post of ambassador to Turkey by new president, James A. Garfield. He left New Mexico on May 30 to accept the job, never to return. Before he left, Wallace authorized a five-hundred-dollar reward for Billy's capture.

Journalism and Billy

Journalism in nineteenth-century America was a very rough-and-tumble, free-for-all game. There were hundreds of newspapers printed all over the country—dailies, weeklies, illustrated, and single sheets. The modern concept of balanced coverage did not exist yet, and papers were free to print anything they liked. And they did, mixing fact, fiction, and opinion without much separation.

In the West, newspapers were the only form of mass communication available. The crusading editor, today a staple of Western lore, took on corrupt politicians, powerful cattle barons, and rampaging outlaws on behalf of the settled, civilized readers. Crusading also made for good copy and boosted circulation. Albert J. Fountain, editor of the *Mesilla Independent*, used his paper to rouse the public against Jesse Evans and the Boys in 1877 and 1878.[2] The outlaws struck back, nearly killing one of Fountain's sons.

After his capture at Stinking Springs, Billy was seldom out of the New Mexico newspapers. He gave interviews and enjoyed the notoriety he gained. Following his spectacular escape from Lincoln and the murders of deputies Bell and Olinger, Billy was blasted in the press as a "young demon," the "terror and disgrace of New Mexico," and a "flagrant violator of every law." The smiling youth was condemned as "malignant and cruel," and having a "spirit as hideous as hell."[3] Behind the overblown rhetoric there was often a grudging admiration of his audacity and courage.[4]

Searching for Billy

Pat Garrett wondered what to do. He had reliable reports Billy was in the Fort Sumner area. He could not believe it. Why would anyone with a death sentence hanging over him remain so close by? Garrett gave Billy credit for more sense than that, but evidence grew that Billy was right where rumor and written news reports had placed him. Inquiries around Fort Sumner confirmed Billy's presence, but no one was certain—or willing to reveal—where he had been hiding.

Garrett sent John Poe to Fort Sumner to investigate. Poe, another former buffalo hunter and lawman from Texas, had been hired by the Panhandle Stock Association as a detective. Poe was a competent lawman, and his abilities led Pat Garrett to swear him in as a Lincoln County deputy sheriff. Since he was unknown around Fort Sumner, his presence might not automatically warn Billy the law was on his trail. Poe lingered in saloons and cultivated local Latino ranchers, but any mention of Billy the Kid provoked only sullen silence.[5]

Poe met Garrett and another reliable deputy, Thomas "Kip" McKinney, at Punta de la Glorietta, about four miles from Fort Sumner. Poe's findings were not concrete, but the lawmen were sure Billy was near. Garrett decided to check with Pete Maxwell, a prominent local rancher. The sheriff may have known of a relationship between Billy and Maxwell's sister Paulita. Maxwell walked a curious line, like a lot of people around Fort Sumner. Not an outlaw himself, he nonetheless kept on good terms with Billy. Willing or not, Garrett felt he could find out something about the Kid from Maxwell.[6]

One Final Showdown

Garrett and his deputies reached the Maxwell ranch at night. On the way, the lawmen stumbled across a man camping. They investigated, and found out the man was an old friend of Poe's who just happened to be in the area. They drank coffee together and went on to the Maxwell place.

Near the house they heard some conversation in Spanish. The lawmen took cover. A figure rose from the shadows. They could not see his face, but he was wearing a shirt, vest, and pants, and had a wide sombrero on his head. Garrett's posse had fired quickly at Stinking Springs and killed Charlie Bowdre, thinking he was Billy in his Mexican hat. This time the lawmen waited to be sure. The dark figure went over a fence and headed for the Maxwell house.[7]

It was Billy. He had been staying nearby with a Latino friend, lying about, reading a newspaper, and generally taking it easy. He grew hungry, and decided to walk to Pete Maxwell's for some beef. Garrett and his men had almost bumped into Billy in the dark.

They were at this point still unsure the man they saw was the Kid, but Garrett was not giving up. The lawmen circled away from the fence and approached Maxwell's house from the opposite direction. There was a porch across the front of the house. Garrett made Poe and McKinney stay at the end of the porch on watch.

The sheriff entered Pete Maxwell's bedroom via the outside door.

Close to midnight, Garrett went to the rancher's bedside and woke him, asking if Billy was in the house. Maxwell, no doubt alarmed by Garrett's looming presence by his bed, admitted the Kid had been there, but he did not know where he was right then.

At that moment Billy came around to the porch. He had a knife in one hand (to carve meat) and his Colt Lightning revolver in the other. He almost ran into John Poe, waiting on the porch. Surprised, Billy leveled his gun at the man he did not recognize.

"Quien es?" he asked. This is Spanish for "Who is it?"[8] Billy backed away, repeating his question.

Poe, a brave man, advanced toward Billy and told him not to be alarmed. Billy retreated to Pete Maxwell's bedroom door, still asking Poe to identify himself. Then he ducked inside the room.[9]

Maxwell and Garrett were still there, in the dark. Billy then asked Maxwell, "Who are those fellows outside, Pete?"

Maxwell said to Garrett, "That's him."

At this point Billy realized someone else was in the room. He called *"Quien es? Quien es?"* again.

At this point Billy realized someone else was in the room. He called *"Quien es? Quien es?"* again.[10]

Garrett drew his gun and fired at the voice. The flare of exploding gunpowder dazzled him in the dark room, but he dodged to one side and fired again. The second

A woodcut of the scene of Billy the Kid's death at the hands of Pat Garrett.

shot was not needed. Garrett's first round had found its mark. Billy collapsed and died.

The sheriff emerged from Maxwell's room. He said to Poe, "That was the Kid that came in here and I think I got him."

Poe did not believe it. He replied, "Pat, the Kid would not come to this place, you have shot the wrong man."[11]

Garrett was rattled by the suddenness of it all, but he declared he knew Billy's voice very well. He was sure he had shot the right man.

Maxwell came out, alarming Poe and nearly getting shot himself. The rancher went for a light. Both he and Pat Garrett identified the dead man as William H. Bonney, alias Billy the Kid. The time was just after midnight, July 14, 1881.

> "That was the Kid that came in here and I think I got him."

A Grave in a Cage

The morning after Billy died, an inquest (a formal legal procedure) was held into the incident. Alejandro Segura, *alcalde* (mayor) of Fort Sumner, presided. The coroner's jury found that William H. Bonney was killed by a gunshot wound inflicted by Sheriff Pat F. Garrett. The sheriff killed Bonney in the pursuit of his lawful duties, so the homicide was justifiable. No one present knew the dead man's real name, Henry McCarty. The Kid had not used his real name in years.

Billy's body was neatly dressed and formally buried in the old military cemetery of Fort Sumner on July 15, 1881. He was laid to rest as "William H. Bonney" beside his old friends Tom O'Folliard and Charlie Bowdre. (Today they share a common headstone). Pat Garrett noted his exact age as twenty-one years, seven months, and twenty-one days.[1]

Garrett's memoir, *The Authentic Life of Billy the Kid*, was actually written by Marshall Ashmun Upson, who as postmaster of Roswell, New Mexico, knew both Garrett and Billy. Garrett supplied the information, and Upson whipped out a readable but not entirely reliable book published in 1882. But what neither Upson nor Garrett related was what happened in the immediate aftermath of Billy's death.

Angry Locals

A large crowd of Pete Maxwell's family and employees gathered around the house when word spread that Billy had been shot. They were angry. One servant pounded Garrett on the chest with her fists, swearing at him for killing her *amigo*. Paulita Maxwell, who some historians suspect was the love of Billy's life, was also deeply upset. Garrett, Poe, and McKinney retreated into the house, afraid that the outpouring of grief for the slain outlaw could turn violent.

Fort Sumner did not take the news of Billy's demise well. Hotheads gathered and there was talk of lynching the sheriff and his men.[2] Garrett avoided violence by remaining at the Maxwell ranch until after the inquest. Once Billy was buried, the anger died down.

Pat Garrett lived another twenty-seven years. He was murdered in 1908, probably because of a dispute with a tenant on his land.[3]

A City Boy in the Wild West?

If there is any key to understanding how a poor Irish boy from New York City became the most famous outlaw of the Wild West, it may lie in the details of the killings for which Billy was responsible. Without a doubt he killed Windy Cahill, Joe Grant, Bob Olinger, J. W. Bell, and most likely Jimmy Carlyle, too. The first three were all known to be bullies who pushed the Kid too far. Bell and Carlyle were innocent men who made the mistake of trusting Billy when he was in desperate straits. All five men therefore made the same mistake: they thought Billy Bonney was not as dangerous as everyone said. Unfortunately, for those men, their mistake cost them dearly.

Why did Henry McCarty turn to a life of crime? Billy seems to have always been searching for a leader to follow. This may have been due to the lack of a father in his life. His own father was a shadowy figure about whom little is known. His stepfather, William Antrim, was too busy prospecting to properly raise Henry.

So Billy gave his loyalty and his fighting skills again and again to dangerous, charismatic leaders. Jesse Evans was no more than a brutal thug. John Tunstall was a robber baron. And Dick Brewer was a vengeful hothead.

Alexander McSween was no inspirational hero, but the Regulators and their cause inspired Billy for a time. When these leaders and their causes failed, Billy was left with just himself.

His judgment failed him. He continued his criminal activities while trying to convince Governor Lew Wallace to grant him amnesty (and Wallace, in an odd way, is another leader Billy might have followed, had he gotten the chance). He returned to Fort Sumner time and again, even when he knew he was being hunted by the law. Many historians have wondered why. Was he attached to the place because he thought of it as home? Did he think his many friendships with the local population would shield him from capture? Or was there another reason—love, in the person of Paulita Maxwell—for which he would not leave New Mexico? Whatever the truth, Billy's attachment to the region cost him his life. Pat Garrett was a determined manhunter, but it did not take a master tracker to find Billy.

All five men therefore made the same mistake: they thought Billy Bonney was not as dangerous as everyone said.

Though gossip and sensational news stories made Billy the leader of an outlaw gang, he never really was. He was too agreeable, too much of a comrade to lead other men. When his criminal colleagues one by one had been killed, captured, or fled, Billy had no one to back him up. He died alone, too dangerous to take alive and too young to understand the need to change his ways.

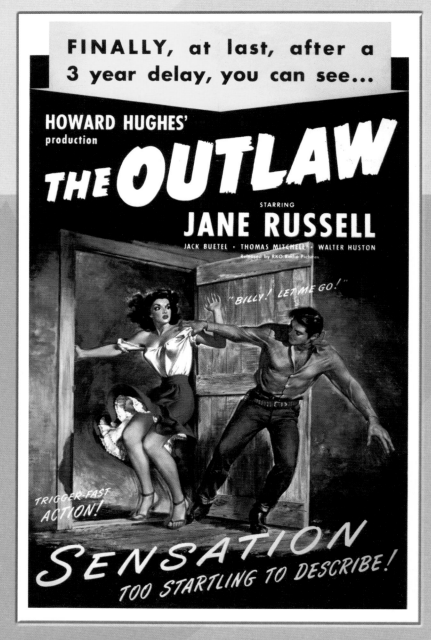

Sensational news stories and gossip further spread the legend of Billy the Kid. Dime novels, plays, books, and movies about the Kid sprouted up everywhere. This is the movie poster for *The Outlaw*, a 1943 film about Billy the Kid.

A Growing Legend

No sooner was Billy dead than the myths about him began to grow anew throughout the West and beyond. Many wild tales had circulated during his life, but his sudden death at such a young age kicked off a whirlwind of outlandish dime novels and sensational "true" stories. In some accounts, he was a modern Robin Hood, battling evil cattle barons and corrupt politicians. In others he was a cold-blooded killer, ready to gun down anyone who blocked his schemes.

Billy was not all of one or the other. He could be generous and charming one moment, mean and merciless the next. In an age when ethnic bigotry was common, he was fair and friendly with the numerous Mexican Americans of his chosen home. They, in turn, idolized the Kid as a sort of knight-errant who stood up to the landlords and cattlemen who trampled their rights and stole their land. Billy reveled in their admiration, and in the worship of other outlaws like Tom O'Folliard. In a sense he became the infamous outlaw people believed he was in order to live up to the praise—and the condemnation—he received.

Despite his fame, in many ways Billy Bonney was the opposite of the idealized Western hero (or a Western villain). He was not tall, he was not taciturn, and he did not command much respect by his presence. His ultimate opponent, Pat Garrett, was more in the mold of a Western hero than Billy, but today "Juan Largo" is remembered as the man who shot Billy the Kid and for little else.

Cheap books and dime novels of the Kid's own day usually portray him as a cold, deadly killer whose guns never missed. Readers of the day may have found that image of Billy admirable, but only as a "good bad man" whose life provided a good moral lesson to others.

The Kid in the Twentieth Century

By the 1920s, most of the people who had actually known Billy were gone, and the real romanticization of Billy the Kid began. In 1926, a Chicago newspaperman, Walter Noble Burns, published a popular book titled The Saga of Billy the Kid. More than any other work, Burns' book furthered the image of the Kid as an American Robin Hood.[4]

It is worth noting that Burns lived in the heyday of Prohibition, when gangsters and bootleggers were glamorized. When the Great Depression began in 1929, banks and big businessmen were widely blamed for the wretched state of the country. The career of Billy the Kid—real and imaginary—had new meaning in the 1930s. Billy was seen as a little guy striking back at the rich. Viewed through the lens of bankruptcy and breadlines, his battles with Jimmy Dolan and the House resonated with many Americans, whether the deeds described by Burns or his imitators were true or not.

The hero worship of Billy the Kid persisted, and grew. Composer Aaron Copland centered his ballet *Billy the Kid* around the mythical Billy Bonney. Drawing heavily on Burns, the ballet depicts Billy as a tragic figure trapped by powerful, sinister men. Somehow Henry

Composer Aaron Copland at his piano in 1960. He centered his ballet, **Billy the Kid,** *on the mythical William H. Bonney.*

McCarty, the real youth who became Billy the Kid, had gotten lost in all the legend-building.

The mythology surrounding Billy took on strange aspects. At the close of his book, Pat Garrett (through Upson) heartily condemned the scavengers who literally wanted a piece of the legend:

> *I have said that the body [of Billy the Kid] was buried in the cemetery at Fort Sumner. I wish to add that it is there to-day intact—skull, fingers, toes, bones and every hair of the head that was buried with the body on that 15th of July, doctors, newspaper editors, and paragraphers to the contrary notwithstanding. Some presuming swindlers have claimed to have the Kid's skull on exhibition,*

Billy the Kid's grave in Fort Sumner, New Mexico. The cage was built around the gravesite to stop people from digging up the remains.

or one of his fingers, or some other portion of his body, and one medical gentleman has persuaded credulous idiots that he has all the bones strung upon wires . . . again I say that the Kid's body lies undisturbed in the grave, and I speak of what I know.[5]

Pilfering the remains of famous dead people is uncommon today. But one form of grave theft persists. Billy's grave marker has been stolen so many times local authorities have enclosed it with an iron railing.[6] The irony of this measure is that now Billy the Kid—a man who escaped from jail so many times—will lie behind bars forever.

CHRONOLOGY

1859 — **September (or possibly November):** Henry McCarty is born in New York City.

1865 — McCarty family, (mother Catherine, sons Henry and Joseph) move to Indiana; Catherine meets Union veteran William H. Antrim.

1870 — The McCartys and Antrim move to Wichita, Kansas; Catherine McCarty contracts tuberculosis.

1873 — **March 1:** William Antrim and Catherine McCarty marry.

1874 — **September 16:** Catherine McCarty dies of TB.

1875 — Henry McCarty arrested in Silver City, New Mexico, for stealing laundry; escapes to Arizona.

1877 — **August 17:** Henry kills "Windy" Cahill in a saloon fight and flees back to New Mexico.

— **September:** Henry, known now as Kid Antrim, arrives in Lincoln County, New Mexico; he joins the Boys gang as William H. Bonney.

— Billy signs on with John Tunstall as a ranch hand and gunfighter.

1878 — **February:** Tunstall is murdered by a posse of Dolan gunmen; Tunstall's loyal hands form a vigilante band called the Regulators.

—**March 31:** The Regulators (including Billy) ambush Sheriff Brady and his deputies in Lincoln; Brady and one deputy are killed.

—**April 4:** The Regulators hunt down "Buckshot" Roberts, a member of the posse that killed Tunstall; Roberts and Regulator chief Dick Brewer are killed.

—**July 15–19:** Three-way battle in Lincoln between the Dolanites, the Regulators, and members of the U.S. Army; Alexander McSween is killed by Dolan's men, and the Regulators are driven out of town; the end of the Lincoln County War.

—**October:** Billy returns to Lincoln; Billy decides to go straight and win a pardon for his past crimes from the new governor, Lew Wallace.

1879 —**February 18:** Billy offers to make peace with his enemies in the Dolan group; while meeting them in Lincoln, lawyer Huston Chapman is murdered by Dolan.

—**March 13:** After a campaign to round up the murderers of Chapman, Governor Wallace receives the first of many letters from Billy, offering evidence about past crimes in New Mexico in exchange for immunity from prosecution.

—**March 17:** Billy and Lew Wallace meet at the home of Justice John Wilson.

—**March 21:** Billy peacefully surrenders to Sheriff Kimbrell.

—**June 17:** Billy and a fellow Regulator, Doc Scurlock, leave Lincoln, breaking their deal with the governor.

1880 —**January 10:** Billy kills Joe Grant in a saloon fight in Fort Sumner.

—**November 2:** Pat F. Garrett is elected sheriff of Lincoln County.

—**November 27:** Billy and his outlaw friends are cornered at the Greathouse ranch by a large posse of lawmen; a local blacksmith named Jimmy Carlyle entered the ranch to negotiate with the outlaws and was killed; the outlaws escape.

—**December 23:** Billy and four other outlaws surrender to Sheriff Pat Garrett.

1881 —**March 30–April 14:** Billy is tried on Federal charges and cleared; he is convicted on local charges of the murder of Sheriff Brady and sentenced to hang.

—**April 28:** Billy escapes and kills deputies Bell and Olinger; he rides out of Lincoln for the last time.

—**July 14:** Billy is shot dead by Garrett at Maxwell's ranch.

—**July 15:** Henry McCarty, alias William H. Bonney, alias Billy the Kid, is buried at Fort Sumner.

CHAPTER NOTES

CHAPTER 1
The Smell of Bacon

1. Robert M. Utley, *Billy the Kid: A Short and Violent Life* (Lincoln, Nebr.: University of Nebraska Bison Books, 1991), p. 24.
2. Bill O'Neal, *The Pimlico Encyclopedia of Western Gunfighters* (London: Pimlico, 1998), p. 202.
3. Pat F. Garrett (ghostwritten by Ashmun Upson), *The Authentic Life of Billy the Kid* (Birmingham, Ala.: Palladium Press, 2007), p. 179.
4. Utley, p. 160.

CHAPTER 2
City Boy

1. Robert M. Utley, *Billy the Kid: A Short and Violent Life* (Lincoln, Nebr.: University of Nebraska Bison Books, 1991), p. 2.
2. Ibid.
3. Jon Tuska, *Billy the Kid, A Bio-Bibliography* (Westport, Conn.: Greenwood Press, 1983), pp. 3–4.
4. Ibid., p. 4.
5. Michael Wallis, *Billy the Kid: The Endless Ride* (New York: W. W. Norton, 2007), pp. 77–78.
6. Ibid., p. 72.
7. "The Left Handed Gun," Internet Movie Database, 2009, <http://www.imdb.com/title/tt0051849/> (March 9, 2009).
8. Utley, pp. 7–8.
9. Tuska, p. 6.
10. Philip J. Rasch, with Allan Radbourne, "The Story of 'Windy' Cahill," in *Trailing Billy the Kid* (Laramie, Wyo.: National Association for Outlaw and Lawman History, 1995), p. 188.

CHAPTER 3

Lincoln County

1. Robert M. Utley, *Billy the Kid: A Short and Violent Life* (Lincoln, Nebr.: University of Nebraska Bison Books, 1991), p. 15.
2. Jon Tuska, *Billy the Kid, A Bio-Bibliography* (Westport, Conn.: Greenwood Press, 1983), p. 9.
3. Michael Wallis, *Billy the Kid: The Endless Ride* (New York: W. W. Norton, 2007), p. 124.
4. Utley, p. 22.
5. Ibid., p. 23.
6. Ibid., p. 26.
7. Wallis, p. 175.
8. Frederick W. Nolan, ed., *The Life and Death of John Henry Tunstall* (Albuquerque, N. Mex.: University of New Mexico Press, 1965), p. 213.
9. Utley, pp. 29–30.

CHAPTER 4

The Regulators

1. Michael Wallis, *Billy the Kid: The Endless Ride* (New York: W. W. Norton, 2007), p. 194.
2. George W. Coe, *Frontier Fighter* (Chicago: Lakeside Press, 1984), pp. 49–50.
3. Joseph G. Rosa, *The Age of the Gunfighter* (New York: Smithmark Publishers, 1993), pp. 54–55, 38–39, 66–67.
4. Frederick Nolan, *The West of Billy the Kid* (Norman, Okla.: University of Oklahoma Press, 1998), p. 108.
5. Ibid., p. 111.
6. Robert M. Utley, *Billy the Kid: A Short and Violent Life* (Lincoln, Nebr.: University of Nebraska Bison Books, 1991), p. 66.
7. Ibid., p. 72.
8. Wallis, p. 203.

CHAPTER 5
War

1. Robert M. Utley, *Billy the Kid: A Short and Violent Life* (Lincoln, Nebr.: University of Nebraska Bison Books, 1991), p. 77.
2. Jon Tuska, *Billy the Kid, A Bio-Bibliography* (Westport, Conn.: Greenwood Press, 1983), p. 38.
3. Utley, p. 82.
4. Ibid., p. 83.
5. Marilyn Watson, "Was Sallie Billy's Girl?" *New Mexico Magazine* (January 1988), pp. 57–66.
6. Michael Wallis, *Billy the Kid: The Endless Ride* (New York: W. W. Norton, 2007), p. 212.
7. Utley, p. 91.
8. Ibid., pp. 213–214.
9. Ibid., p. 122.
10. Philip J. Rasch, "Five Days of Battle," in *The Billy the Kid Reader* (Norman, Okla.: University of Oklahoma Press, 2007), pp. 279–280.
11. Ibid., p. 280.
12. Wallis, p. 216.

CHAPTER 6
The Governor

1. Jon Tuska, *Billy the Kid, A Bio-Bibliography* (Westport, Conn.: Greenwood Press, 1983), p. 13.
2. Michael Wallis, *Billy the Kid: The Endless Ride* (New York: W. W. Norton, 2007), p. 225.
3. Ibid., p. 226.
4. Robert M. Utley, *Billy the Kid: A Short and Violent Life* (Lincoln, Nebr.: University of Nebraska Bison Books, 1991), p. 116.
5. Ibid., p. 117.
6. Tuska, p. 69.
7. Utley, p. 121.
8. "James Dolan—Bad Hombre in the Lincoln County War," Legends of America, 2003–2009, <http://www.legendsofamerica.com/we-jamesdolan.html> (March 9, 2009).

CHAPTER 7
On the Run

1. Robert M. Utley, *Billy the Kid: A Short and Violent Life* (Lincoln, Nebr.: University of Nebraska Bison Books, 1991), p. 126.
2. J. R. Sanders, "Faro: Favorite Gambling Game of the Frontier," *Wild West Magazine*, October 1996.
3. "Faro or 'Bucking the Tiger,'" The Gentleman's Page, n.d., <http://www.lahacal.org/gentleman/faro.html> (March 9, 2009).
4. For Henry Brown's career after New Mexico, *The Gunfighters* (Alexandria, Va.: Time-Life Books, 1974), pp. 110–113.
5. Utley, p. 127.
6. Jon Tuska, *Billy the Kid, A Bio-Bibliography* (Westport, Conn.: Greenwood Press, 1983), p. 72.
7. Michael Wallis, *Billy the Kid: The Endless Ride* (New York: W. W. Norton, 2007), p. 234.
8. Ibid., p. 230.
9. Utley, p. 129.
10. Ibid., p. 134.
11. Tuska, pp. 73–76.
12. The actual vote count was 320 for Garrett and 179 for Kimbrell, in Leon Metz, *Pat Garrett: The Story of a Western Lawman* (Norman, Okla.: University of Oklahoma Press, 1973), p. 57.

CHAPTER 8
Caught at Last

1. Robert M. Utley, *Billy the Kid: A Short and Violent Life* (Lincoln, Nebr.: University of Nebraska Bison Books, 1991), pp. 142–143.
2. Pat F. Garrett (ghostwritten by Ashmun Upson), *The Authentic Life of Billy the Kid* (Birmingham, Ala.: Palladium Press, 2007), pp. 137–138.
3. Utley, p. 145.
4. Jon Tuska, *Billy the Kid, A Bio-Bibliography* (Westport, Conn.: Greenwood Press, 1983), p. 84.
5. Utley, p. 148.
6. Ibid., p. 153.

7. Garrett, p. 169.
8. Ibid., pp. 171–173.

CHAPTER 9
Follow Me No Longer

1. Jon Tuska, *Billy the Kid, A Bio-Bibliography* (Westport, Conn.: Greenwood Press, 1983), p. 89.
2. Ibid.
3. Ibid., p. 90.
4. Pat F. Garrett (ghostwritten by Ashmun Upson), *The Authentic Life of Billy the Kid* (Birmingham, Ala.: Palladium Press, 2007), p. 187.
5. Robert M. Utley, *Billy the Kid: A Short and Violent Life* (Lincoln, Nebr.: University of Nebraska Bison Books, 1991), p. 172.
6. Ibid., p. 174.
7. Garrett, p. 189.
8. Ibid., pp. 191–192.
9. Bill O'Neal, *The Pimlico Encyclopedia of Western Gunfighters* (London: Pimlico, 1998), pp. 202–203.
10. Ibid., p. 5.
11. Garrett, p. 202.

CHAPTER 10
"Who is it? Who is it?"

1. Robert M. Utley, *Billy the Kid: A Short and Violent Life* (Lincoln, Nebr.: University of Nebraska Bison Books, 1991), p. 187.
2. Ibid., p. 172.
3. Ibid., pp. 183–184.
4. Pat F. Garrett (ghostwritten by Ashmun Upson), *The Authentic Life of Billy the Kid* (Birmingham, Ala.: Palladium Press, 2007), note C, p. 196.
5. Ibid., p. 190.
6. Ibid., p. 213.
7. Ibid., p. 214.
8. Utley, pp. 192–193.

9. John W. Poe, "The Killing of Billy the Kid," in Frederick Nolan, ed., *The Billy the Kid Reader* (Norman, Okla.: University of Oklahoma Press, 2007), p. 336.
10. Garrett, p. 216.
11. Poe, p. 337.

CHAPTER 11
A Grave in a Cage

1. Pat F. Garrett (ghostwritten by Ashmun Upson), *The Authentic Life of Billy the Kid* (Birmingham, Ala.: Palladium Press, 2007), p. 219.
2. Robert M. Utley, *Billy the Kid: A Short and Violent Life* (Lincoln, Nebr.: University of Nebraska Bison Books, 1991), p. 195.
3. Bill O'Neal, *The Pimlico Encyclopedia of Western Gunfighters* (London: Pimlico, 1998), pp. 118–119.
4. Utley, p. 200.
5. Garrett, pp. 219–220.
6. "Tourist Attractions," Fort Sumner Chamber of Commerce, 2002, <http://www.ftsumnerchamber.com/tourist.htm> (March 9, 2009).

GLOSSARY

buffalo hunter—Professional hunters that killed thousands of buffalo from 1850 to 1880.

cattle baron—A businessman who amassed huge herds of cattle on enormous parcels of land.

deputy—A law officer, usually under the authority of a sheriff or marshal.

lynching—An illegal killing by hanging by mob action.

marshal—Either a town law enforcement officer, or a federal law officer responsible for enforcement of federal laws across a wide area.

monopoly—When every business in a certain field or region is owned by a single person or company.

outlaw—A criminal who has been declared "outside the law," by authorities. In this case, ordinary rules of arrest and due process may be waived and the criminal can be detained or killed by anyone.

posse—A band of men organized to assist law enforcement officers in catching criminals.

ranch—A farm for raising livestock, especially cattle, horses, or sheep.

regulator—A free citizen who bands together with others to restore law and order.

rustler—A cattle or horse thief.

vigilante—A self-appointed law enforcement officer.

FURTHER READING

Books

Blackwood, Gary L. *Outlaws*. New York: Benchmark Books, 2002.

Forty, Sandra. *New Mexico Past and Present*. San Diego, Calif.: Thunder Bay Press, 2009.

Harmon, Daniel E. *Billy the Kid*. Philadelphia: Chelsea House Publishers, 2001.

Healy, Nick. *Billy the Kid: Legends of the West*. Mankato, Minn.: Creative Education, 2006.

Stefoff, Rebecca. *The Wild West*. New York: Marshall Cavendish, 2007.

Internet Addresses

About Billy the Kid
   <http://www.aboutbillythekid.com/>

Badhombres—Billy the Kid
   <http://www.badhombres.com/outlaws/
   billy-the-kid.htm>

The Billy the Kid Museum
   <http://www.billythekidmuseumfortsumner.com/>

INDEX